GIVE 'EM HELL, HARRY!

A DOCUMENTARY DRAMA
of the
TRUMAN WHITE HOUSE YEARS

by Carl E. Bolte, Jr.

To President Harry S. Truman:

A Great Missourian . . .

A Great President . . .

A Great American.

CEB, Jr.

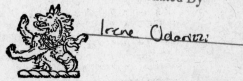

SAMUEL FRENCH, INC.

25 WEST 45TH STREET   N

7623 SUNSET BOULEVARD   HO

LONDON

D1057330

The premiere of GIVE 'EM HELL, HARRY! was in Kansas City at the Music Hall on May 7, 1970, the eve of President Truman's eighty-sixth Birthday. The Kansas City Junior Chamber of Commerce presented it as a benefit performance for the Kansas City Philharmonic Orchestra. It created quite a stir here in Truman Country. Honorary Chairmen for the event included former President Lyndon B. Johnson, Missouri Senator Stuart Symington, former Kansas Senator Harry Darby, Congressman Dr. Durward Hall, Missouri Lieutenant Governor William S. Morris, and some sixteen other leading citizens of the community.

CHARACTERS

PRESIDENT TRUMAN .... *George C. Berry*

BILL .... *Wilbur Goodseal*

BESS TRUMAN .... *Anita Van Wye*

MARGARET TRUMAN .... *Naomi Hembree*

MRS. TRUMAN .... *Helen Venneberg*
   (the President's mother)

ALSO FEATURING:

  *Bradley Barr, Richard Bowzer, Frank Carella, John
Carey, Thomas Clark, William Cosgrove, Alice
Elliott, Maralyn Elliott, Harold Foster, Larry
Jay, Louis (Dutch) Meyers, David Odegard,
Cathy Parks, Donald Quinn, Albert Wallace*

4

GIVE 'EM HELL, HARRY!

ACT ONE

SCENE 1

SCENE: *There are twelve chairs from Upstage to Downstage Right. Six chairs are Upstage to Downstage Left, with the Downstage chair slightly separated from the others. Upstage, slightly Left of Center is the Presidential desk with a chair Upstage of it and two chairs flanking it. The American and Presidential flags are at either side and Upstage of the desk. A smaller desk and chair are at Upstage Left, occupied by* MATT CONNELLY, *who sits facing into Left wings. A lectern is at Downstage Left. With only a few exceptions as noted, the Stage remains set in this manner throughout the production. All actors, except* HST, *are on Stage [see "Production Notes," pages 85–88, at the end of the script].*

TIME: *At present.*

AT RISE: *The Stage-Right desk chair is slightly Downstage of desk. It is occupied by a stunned but controlled* ELEANOR ROOSEVELT, *who is being consoled by Press Secretary* STEVE EARLY. *After an eight-second pause,* BILL *rises solemnly and quietly, crosses to lectern.* BILL *is an intelligent, if not particularly well-educated Negro of perhaps sixty. He is valet/servant/friend/confidant to the President. He speaks in a quiet voice befitting his pronouncement.*

5

BILL. On April 12, 1945, Franklin Delano Roosevelt, the thirty-second President of the United States, suffered a fatal stroke in Warm Springs, Georgia.

(BILL *crosses, sits. Vice President* HARRY S. TRUMAN *enters, Stage Left, crosses quickly to* EARLY, *who crosses to meet him. They shake hands, speak in solemn tones.*)

HST. Steve. I came as quick as I could.

EARLY. I still can't believe it, Harry. Less than an hour ago.

HST. We looked to him. FDR meant so much to all of us. What will the country do without him?

EARLY. You'll have to decide that now.

HST. (*Sees* MRS. ROOSEVELT, *crosses to her, bends down, takes her hands.* EARLY *follows.*) Mrs. Roosevelt, is there anything I can do for you? (*Pause.*)

MRS. ROOSEVELT. Is there anything I can do for you, because it is up to you now.

HST. No one could ever replace him. I will try to do what he would have done.

MRS. ROOSEVELT. Yes, I'm sure you will, Harry. (*Vacantly, staring out at fourth wall, rising.*) I'm sure you will. (EARLY *escorts* MRS. ROOSEVELT *to her chair, stands beside her. Speaker of the House* SAM RAYBURN *and Senator* HARLEY KILGORE *rise, cross to* HST.)

RAYBURN. I saw FDR just before he left for Warm Springs. Now he's gone. It's up to you, Harry.

KILGORE. What are you going to do?

HST. The only thing I can: continue his programs. Where do we get a man like the President?

KILGORE. He was a great man. I'm glad he had you. And I'm glad we've got you now, Harry.

HST. (*Crossing Downstage of* RAYBURN, *earnestly takes* KILGORE'S *arm, pleads.*) Harley, pray for me.

KILGORE. I will, Harry. We all will.

(BESS, MARGARET, *and* MAMA TRUMAN *rise, cross to*
    HST *escorted by* EARLY. HST *crosses to them,*
    takes both hands of each lady. RAYBURN *and*
    KILGORE *confer quietly.*)

BESS. We hurried over after we got your call.

HST. I'm glad you got here in time for this, Bess.

MARGARET. Hello, Daddy.

HST. Hello, Margie. Hello, Mama.

BESS. Poor Mrs. Roosevelt. My heart goes out to her.

HST. Yes. She's taking it very well. She's a courageous woman.

RAYBURN. (*Crossing quietly to* HST.) Harry, Chief Justice Stone is here— (STONE *rises.*) to administer the oath whenever you are ready.

HST. Is any man ever ready? No, I'm not ready, but I'll do my best to keep my feet on the ground. (HST *and* STONE *cross to Downstage Center.* HST *puts left hand on the Bible, both raise their right hands.*)

STONE. I . . .

HST. I, Harry S. Truman . . .

STONE. Do solemnly swear . . .

HST. Do solemnly swear . . .

STONE. That I will faithfully execute the office of President of the United States . . .

HST. That I will faithfully execute the office of President of the United States . . .

STONE. And will to the best of my ability . . .

HST. And will to the best of my ability . . .

STONE. Preserve, protect and defend the Constitution of the United States.

HST. Preserve, protect and defend the Constitution of the United States. (*President* HARRY S. TRUMAN *takes Bible, kisses it.* STONE *shakes his hand,* BESS *crosses Downstage, kisses* HST *on the cheek, as does* MARGARET *and* MRS. TRUMAN. *Others cross, shake his hand, wish him well.* RAYBURN *crosses to* MRS. TRUMAN.)

RAYBURN. This must be a proud moment for you, Mrs. Truman.

MRS. TRUMAN. (*Thoughtful, quiet, almost vacant.*) I cannot really be glad my son is President because I am sorry that President Roosevelt is dead. If he had been voted in, I would be out waving the flag. But it doesn't seem right.

(KILGORE *sets chair to Right of desk. All except* HST *cross to chairs, sit.* REPORTERS *rise, cross to Center Stage as* HST *crosses to meet them. They are brash, hurried, unfeeling.* HST's *irritation of them builds during these lines.*)

FIRST REPORTER. Mr. President . . .

HST. I wish you didn't have to call me that.

SECOND REPORTER. What are your plans?

HST. I'd rather not discuss it now.

FIRST REPORTER. Will you continue the New Deal?

HST. This is not the time or the place to . . .

SECOND REPORTER. Have you scheduled a press conference?

HST. No. I have asked the cabinet to stay with me. That's all I wish to say at . . .

FIRST REPORTER. When will you move into the White House?

HST. After Mrs. Roosevelt has had ample time. I will not discuss any further questions you ask in such poor taste. (REPORTERS *cross, sit.* HST *solemn, alone, crosses Downstage to apron. He kneels, bows his head, then looks up, closes his eyes, clasps his hands in front of him, prays earnestly.*) Oh, Almighty God; help me to be, to think, to do what is right because it is right; make me truthful, honest, and honorable in all things without thought of reward to me. Let me be charitable, forgiving and patient with my fellowmen—to understand their shortcomings as Thou understandest mine. Amen.

(*BLACKOUT. HST crosses Upstage to desk, sits.*)

Scene 2

BILL *rises, crosses to lectern. His speech changes the solemn mood to casual, easy, matter-of-fact.*

BILL. There he was, the thirty-third President of your United States. The former Senator, who didn't want to be Senator at all. He went to Washington feeling inadequate. His Missouri drawl had an apology: "I am ignorant about everything worth knowing." Then he hated to leave the Senate ten years later. But his early doubters now recognized that Harry Truman was a pretty darn good man.

He's the former Vice President, who didn't want that office either. But he said, reluctantly: "I'll do what the President wants." Now he was taking over after the tragic death of Mr. Roosevelt who picked him as his successor.

Harry S. Truman has been questioned, second-guessed, and criticized. He has been cussed at, lied about, and damned. Even his top Democratic aides had a standard phrase, behind his back: "The *President* wouldn't do it that way." But he has been widely praised, too.

I saw it happen. I saw the history made. I worked for him here in the White House. I opened the door for his visitors, I brought him his newspaper, I ran his errands.

There have been lots of words written about him. They say things like "only in America" and "from plow to President." They call him "the common man." He was common, all right. He was arrogant, cocky, religious, friendly—he was human. That's why people liked him. He was one of us. The kind of fellow, President or not, that seemed sort of, well, right, to call by his first name.

I understood him. Most people didn't then, but they are finally realizing what I've known all along: that give-em-hell, Harry, the man from Independence, was a sure-enough great President.

His first official appearance— (McKELLAR *and* RAYBURN *rise, cross to Downstage Right, talk quietly.*) after President Roosevelt's funeral, was when he spoke to a Joint Sesssion of Congress, escorted by Senator McKellar and Speaker of the House Rayburn. (BILL *crosses, sits.* McKELLAR *and* RAYBURN *look out at fourth wall, speak solemnly.*)

RAYBURN. I've never seen the House so quiet. Or with this air of gloom, Ken.

McKELLAR. Nearly 600 here, Sam, and hardly a whisper.

RAYBURN. Wish we didn't need this joint session. Well, are we ready?

McKELLAR. The chamber seems to be in order. I'll get Harry. (McKELLAR *crosses slightly Upstage Left, as HST meets him crossing toward lectern.* RAYBURN *crosses to far Left beside lectern. They flank HST as he goes to lectern, immediately starts speaking.*)

HST. Mr. Speaker . . .

RAYBURN. (*Quietly, steps close to him.*) Just a minute, Harry. Let me introduce you. (HST *backs away as* RAYBURN *steps behind lectern.*) The President of the United States. (HST *steps behind lectern.* RAYBURN *crosses to Stage Left of it.*)

HST. Mr. Speaker, President of the Senate, ladies and gentlemen. It is with heavy heart that I stand before you. Tragic fate has thrust upon us grave responsibilities. We must carry on. Our departed leader looked forward and moved forward. That is what he would want us to do. This is what America must do.

I pledge to carry out the war and peace policies of President Roosevelt. We will continue in our demand for unconditional surrender from our enemies.

At this moment I have in my heart a prayer; I ask only to be a good and faithful servant of my Lord and my people.

(*BLACKOUT. HST crosses Upstage to desk, sits. McKellar and Rayburn cross to chairs, sit.*)

Scene 3

BILL *rises, crosses to lectern.*

BILL. How can you *not* like a man like that? People knew he was trying, and if they weren't on his side, at least they felt he wasn't all Missouri mule.

The White House in the days that followed was far different from what it had been. It was old home week. The man at home was as casual as if he was welcoming a visitor on his front porch, like when his aide, General Harry Vaughan, came to the office, he told him to pull up the other rocker and set a spell.

VAUGHAN. (*Laughing.*) And he said to the old maid: "Honey, you won't understand if I draw you a picture."

HST. (*He and* VAUGHAN *laugh.*) That's a good story, Harry.

VAUGHAN. Tell it to Bess. She'd get a kick out of it.

HST. You know who'd get kicked. I told her your joke about the big game hunter who got lost at the zoo. When I had to explain it to her, she walked out.

VAUGHAN. I heard John Snyder tell one the other . . . (*White House Appointments Secretary* MATT CONNELLY, *rises, crosses to desk.*)

MATT. Pardon me, Mr. President.

VAUGHAN. Why, Matt Connelly, how do you like your new job as Appointments secretary?

MATT. Fine, General.

HST. What is it, Matt?

MATT. You've got a busy morning. You know how it was yesterday, sir, and Secretary Anderson is waiting to see you.

HST. (*Resigned.*) Okay. You know, Harry, we had over 400 customers in here. Well, Matt, let's get the store open.

VAUGHAN. (*Rises.*) See you later, Mr. President.

HST. Come on, *General!*

VAUGHAN. (*Hitting him on the arm in a friendly manner.*) All right, *Harry.* (VAUGHAN *and* MATT *cross to chairs, sit. Secretary of Agriculture* CLINTON P. ANDERSON *rises, crosses to desk.*)

ANDERSON. Good morning, Mr. President.

HST. Morning, Clinton. (HST *rises, shakes his hand.* ANDERSON *sits.*) How's everything down on the farm?

ANDERSON. We're trying. Harry, I need your opinion about problems on the feed grain parity.

HST. What do you think?

ANDERSON. Well, if we recommend it, Congress might balk at the rest of the program.

HST. Does that mean yes or no?

ANDERSON. No.

HST. Then don't do it. Damn it, Clint, you're not secretary of agriculture to have me make every decision in your department.

ANDERSON. I know that, sir, but . . .

HST. Don't come to see me every time the price of corn drops two cents. You've got the authority. Use it.

ANDERSON. (*Rises.*) I will.

HST. But keep me advised. I was asked about your wool tariff statement the other day and I didn't know what the hell you had said.

ANDERSON. I thought we talked about it.

HST. No we hadn't. Bring it up in cabinet meeting.

Or write me a memo. I've got to know what the team is doing.

ANDERSON. I'll keep you better informed, Harry. (*He crosses to chair, sits.* HST *picks up mail.* MATT *rises, crosses to desk.*)

MATT. Senator Fulbright is here, sir.

HST. (*Looking at letter.*) Tell him to keep his pants on.

MATT. (*Toward* FULBRIGHT'S *chair, loudly.*) Senator, the President says, uh, just a minute.

HST. Matt, did you know that this is National Pickle Week?

MATT. It's what, sir?

HST. National Pickle Week. They want me to do something to celebrate it. What do I do?

MATT. Eat one, I guess. I'm glad that's your problem.

HST. I'll write and tell 'em I'm in a pickle all year long. (*He puts down letter.*) Well, send in Fulbright.

MATT. (*Toward* FULBRIGHT'S *chair.* FULBRIGHT *rises.*) The President will see you, Senator. (*He crosses to chair, sits. Senator* FULBRIGHT *crosses to desk, shakes hands with* HST, *sits.*)

HST. Hello, Bill.

FULBRIGHT. If I can take just a minute of your time, Mr. President.

HST. Sure. How are things on The Hill?

FULBRIGHT. All right. How do you feel about the resolution?

HST. (*Pointedly.*) That's the *Fulbright* Resolution, I believe.

FULBRIGHT. Uh, yes. The only way we can win the peace is . . .

HST. What peace?

FULBRIGHT. Well, the end of the war is on the horizon.

HST. Is it? You've got the best foresight I know of.

FULBRIGHT. Of course it is. Japan is the next invasion.

HST. It's a hell of a bumpy road. Japan won't be easy.

FULBRIGHT. (*Less patient, less respectful.*) Nobody thinks they're a pushover, Harry. But we've got to be ready with an international organization that will make this the last war. The world can't fight another one.

HST. You were our representative at the Paris Peace Conference. That mission went under like a covered wagon in quicksand.

FULBRIGHT. I did every possible thing I could in those sessions.

HST. Maybe we'd have gotten your best efforts if we'd have called it the *Fulbright* Peace Conference.

FULBRIGHT. We'd have achieved no better results if it was called the *Truman* Peace Conference, and you had been there.

HST. Don't bet on that, Bill.

FULBRIGHT. The fact remains, Mr. President. We need the United Nations. If the U. S. leads, the rest of the world will follow. (*Pause.*) Your silence doesn't mean that you are against the UN, does it?

HST. (*Rises, crosses in front of desk.*) Bill, damn it, my first decision fifteen minutes after I took this office was to go ahead with the establishment of the United Nations. You don't think your idea is new to me, do you?

FULBRIGHT. (*Rises, indecisive.*) Well, from the way you talked . . .

HST. There isn't anybody more pro UN than I am, including you. Here's the speech I'm making to the delegation by radio. Now do you know where I stand? (*He and* FULBRIGHT *look at each other;* HST *crosses to Stage Right, exits.* MATT *rises, crosses to desk.*)

MATT. Mr. President? (*He looks around.*) Where did he go?

FULBRIGHT. Out there. (*He points to right wings, shrugs, resigned.*) In FDR's time we'd come in here depressed and go out buoyant. Now I get the feeling that he doesn't know what I'm talking about. (*He crosses to chair, sits. Two* LADIES *rise.* MATT *speaks to them.*)

MATT. Come in, ladies. The President will be right back.

(LADIES *nervously cross to in front of left side of desk.* FIRST LADY *carries a box of strawberries. They stand uneasily, whisper to each other.* MATT *crosses, sits.* HST *enters, Stage Right, is surprised to see them, crosses toward desk and shakes hands with them warmly.*)

HST. Well, well! I didn't know I'd have the pleasure of being called on by two ladies this morning. Have a seat.

FIRST LADY. (*Embarrassed, giggles, remains standing.*) Mr. President, I'm Mrs. Young, and this is Mrs. Waters. We're from the Strawberry Growers Association of Louisiana, and we'd like to present you with the first of our new crop this year.

HST. Why, thank you very much. (*She hands box to* HST, *who looks at them.*) They're better-looking berries than I used to grow. (LADIES *laugh nervously.*)

FIRST LADY. Uh, well. We hope you like them.

HST. You bet we will. I'll tell Mrs. Truman that strawberry shortcake is a must for dinner tonight. There won't be any left for tomorrow.

SECOND LADY. Yes, sir, there will, Mr. President Truman. That man made us leave the other thirty-one boxes out there.

FIRST LADY. Well, thank you, Mr. President.

HST. Not at all. Now you come back again. (LADIES *cross, sit.* MATT *crosses to desk.* HST *sits on Down-*

stage side of desk.) Matt, what in the devil do we do with all those strawberries?

MATT. Well, sir, uh, Mrs. Connelly and I have always enjoyed . . .

HST. Let's share the wealth.

MATT. Thank you, sir.

HST. Right. Send 'em over to the St. Vincent's orphans home. Those poor kids will like 'em.

MATT. (*Disappointed.*) Uh, yes, sir.

(*BLACKOUT.* HST *crosses, sits at desk.* MATT *crosses to chair, sits.*)

SCENE 4

BILL *rises, crosses to lectern.* ED *crosses Upstage of backdrop for Scene 5.*

BILL. From the amount of time and hard work he put in, there wasn't much that the old man didn't know. What he didn't know, he found out. Truman had lived on Pennsylvania Avenue only two short weeks when he called for his Secretary of War, Henry L. Stimson. (STIMSON *rises.*) And when he called, brother, you came! (*He crosses, sits.* STIMSON *crosses to desk.* HST *rises, shakes his hand.*)

HST. Good morning, Henry. (*Both sit.*)

STIMSON. How was your trip home, Mr. President?

HST. Too short. Don't tell the taxpayers that I like my big white house in Missouri better than theirs.

STIMSON. I'll keep it a secret.

HST. You already keep more secrets from me than Bess does. Henry, what is this money-eater that nobody will tell me about?

STIMSON. I'm not sure I understand.

HST. You must think I'm a bad security risk. Haven't I proved I'm trustworthy? (*He leans forward, kids confidentially, crosses his heart.*) Cross my heart, I won't tell.

STIMSON. I'm sorry, Harry, but I still don't understand.

HST. This Manhattan Project. (*Rises slowly, crosses in front of desk, sits on it.*) I've known about it for a long time. Or rather, I haven't. When I was in the Senate, I heard of this billion-dollar operation, and sent an investigator up to check it.

STIMSON. Oh, yes. I remember very well.

HST. You should. You told me it was a sensitive topmost secret. I called my man off and told you that I didn't want to know any more about it.

STIMSON. I'm glad our security has been that good. (*Concerned about how that remark sounded.*) Oh, I didn't mean it that way, Harry.

HST. (*Laughs.*) I know how you meant it.

STIMSON. Then Roosevelt never told you?

HST. No. Will you quit beating around the bush?

STIMSON. All right. (*Rises, crosses to Down Right Center Stage.*) It started modestly. Then it got to be a very important experiment. Since 1939, our scientists have been working on atomic disintegration, and . . .

HST. Atomic what?

STIMSON. It's called atomic disintegration.

HST. What's it do? (*He crosses Downstage to* STIMSON.) Distintegrate the atoms, like it sounds?

STIMSON. I'm no scientist, but it's a split, of the atoms of an element. It can be used in bombs which have a tremendous capacity.

HST. Is it perfected yet?

STIMSON. It is nearing that stage, they think.

HST. Can we speed it up?

STIMSON. It is moving as fast as possible.

HST. Then let's give it every priority. Our men need all the arsenal we can deliver.

STIMSON. We are. This atomic material is unbelievable as a potential weapons system.

MATT. (*He rises, crosses to desk.*) Mr. President, there are two gentlemen here from . . .

HST. (*Waving* MATT *away.*) Not now, Matt. See that nobody interrupts us.

MATT. Yes, sir. (*He crosses, sits.*)

HST. About this atom weapon. How can it be used?

STIMSON. Strictly, I'm told, as an aerial bomb. The prediction is that one atomic charge will pack the same explosive power as 10,000 tons of TNT.

HST. You mean ten tons?

STIMSON. No. Ten thousand tons. Its full potential is not really known.

HST. (*Incredibly.*) That's unbelievable. Henry, that's a hell of a thing! A weapon that big would shorten the war, wouldn't it?

STIMSON. In all probability, it would end it. The price, of course, would be indiscriminate destruction.

HST. You mean of a larger area than you want to destroy?

STIMSON. Yes.

HST. Why? Why can't it be pin-pointed like a conventional bomb? Our bombadiers can . . . (*He looks around.*) knock this room out without raising dust through the rest of the White House.

STIMSON. It's too big to be controlled. It's hard to comprehend because it is so much bigger than anything the world has ever seen. A physicist explained it to me, that if it were dropped on the Pentagon two miles away, it would destroy the White House, too. Harry, it could blow your Independence, Missouri off the map.

HST. So, in other words, it destroys a military target, and everything else around it?

STIMSON. That's what they say. If it works.

HST. *If?* There isn't any assurance that it will?

STIMSON. This atomic power is still an experiment.

The Germans have been developing it, but our intelligence says they aren't close to a stage of readiness.

HST. Thank God. It is horrendous, isn't it. Blow up the whole town of Independence.

STIMSON. Shall I tell the Manhattan people anything, Harry?

HST. Tell them full speed. Henry, keep me informed on this. If it will shorten the war, or end it, we've got to have it. If there was some way to use just a little of that damn awesome power.

STIMSON. I wish there were, Harry. Is that all?

HST. (*Not hearing, looking vacantly out at fourth wall.*) To have a weapon like this and not use it is unthinkable. To kill all that it would kill is . . . (STIMSON, *seeing that his presence is no longer required, quietly crosses to chair, sits. HST doesn't know he is alone.*) What would Roosevelt do? No President ever had to make such a decision. It requires a lot of conscience-searching, doesn't it, Henry. A lot of asking God what to do.

(*BLACKOUT. HST crosses to desk. Sits.*)

SCENE 5

BILL *rises, crosses to lectern.*

BILL. You know, it's an awful job to be President. He was finding that out, too. It was a good thing that he could get away now and then to Independence and be with the people he liked best. Home folks he called them. His old neighbors, his kind of people. (*He crosses to chair, sits. ED enters, Stage Left, crosses several steps, as CHARLIE rises, crosses several steps to Right Center Stage. ED yells across at him.*)

ED. Hey, Charlie?

CHARLIE. Huh?

ED. Harry's home.

CHARLIE. (*Crossing to* ED.) The hell he is!

ED. The hell he ain't! Didn't you see that crowd down at the depot? He come in on his private train.

CHARLIE. Harry own the train?

ED. Naw, they just loan it to him while he's President.

CHARLIE. 'Member when he was workin' for the Santa Fe, on the section gang? He couldn't even afford to ride one then.

ED. None of us could in them days. Be mighty good to have somebody in the old Wallace place again. (ED *takes* CHARLIE'S *arm, tries to pull him to Stage Left.* CHARLIE *won't follow.*) Let's go over. I'd like to see him.

CHARLIE. He ain't got time for us, Ed. He's President.

ED. He's Harry, ain't he? The day come when he don't want to see his old friends from the lodge and the legion, then he ain't Harry. (HST *rises, crosses Downstage.*)

CHARLIE. Nope. He's too busy. Imagine us havin' a President right here from Independence.

ED. Yeah. And he's showin' some o' them smart-ass east people a thing or two, too.

CHARLIE. Doin' a fine job, but who'd of ever thought you'd see ol' Harry as President?

HST. (*He crosses between them, carrying a cane, has the look of a happy and relaxed man.*)

HST. Even Harry didn't think so. (ED *and* CHARLIE *look up, startled and embarrassed.*) Hi, Ed, Charlie. (HST *shakes hands with them.*) Good to see you both.

ED. Uh, yes, sir, yes, sir, Harry, I mean President.

HST. Hey, let a fellow come home and relax, will you? (*All laugh.* HST *waves and speaks to fourth wall.*) Hello there, Al. (*He speaks to* CHARLIE.) How's your farm?

CHARLIE. Right good. The wheat ought to make

better'n thirty bushel. You been out south to your place yet?

HST. No, and it doesn't look like I'll have time this trip. Wish I could. I miss that farm.

ED. (*Confidentially to* HST, *pointing to left wings.*) Who's that feller back there lookin' around at ev'er-body?

HST. That's Nick, my shadow. If you're President, he has to follow you everywhere. I'd like to get rid of him.

CHARLIE. (*Confidentially.*) Want us to do it, Harry?

HST. (*Laughs.*) No, boys. I mean that I get tired of a secret service man looking over my shoulder all the time.

ED. How does it feel to be President?

HST. It's like riding a tiger. You have to keep on riding him, or be swallowed. (*All laugh.*)

CHARLIE. Do you like it?

HST. I liked being a Senator. But if I'd had any idea that Mr. Roosevelt was going to die, I never would have accepted the nomination for Vice Presi-dent. (HST *waves, speaks to fourth wall.*) Hello, Jim, Martha. Glad to see you. Say, Ed, have you been . . .

(TEENAGE GIRL *rises, crosses between* ED *and* HST.)

GIRL. Would you sign my autograph book, please, Mr. President?

HST. (*Takes book she presents.*) I will, if you'll tell me your name.

GIRL. It's Margaret.

HST. Why, I've got a daughter named Margaret.

GIRL. I know. Her picture was in the paper last week. Is she going to marry that fellow?

HST. (*Laughs.*) I'll let you know as soon as I find out myself. (*He writes in book, speaks to* ED.) This is what I miss—visiting with home folks instead of having to entertain some high monkey-monk from some-place.

ED. We sure miss havin' you around here, too.

HST. (*Hands book to* GIRL.) Here you are.

GIRL. Thank you. (*She reads book.*) "To another very pretty girl named Margaret." Oh, thank you, Mr. President. (*She takes his arm, pulls him down to where she can kiss him on the cheek.* HST *is delighted and touched.* GIRL *runs to Stage Right, exits.* MATT *rises, cross to* HST. REPORTERS *rise, cross to Down-stage Right, confer.*)

HST. I get lonely to come back, but once or twice a year is all that they'll let me out of the White House.

MATT. Mr. President, the press wants to talk to you.

HST. Matt, can't a man have a day off?

MATT. Doesn't look like it, sir. Don't forget what we discussed the other night.

HST. About what?

MATT. Reporters questions. If they hit a subject you aren't ready to discuss yet, tell them "no comment." It might save you a lot of embarrassment later.

HST. Matt, you know me better than that. When was the last time I didn't have a comment?

MATT. Probably sixty-one years ago, sir. (HST *crosses to* REPORTERS, *very much at ease.* MATT *follows closely, followed by* CHARLIE *and* ED, *who enjoy seeing their friend at a press conference.* REPORTERS *write in notebooks.*)

FIRST REPORTER. Are you glad to be home, Mr. President?

HST. You bet! It makes a man wonder why he ever left.

SECOND REPORTER. Then you wish you weren't President?

HST. I didn't say that, and don't print it that way. Incidentally, boys, are we off the record? (REPORTERS *nod, comment affirmatively.*)

THIRD REPORTER. Are you going right back to Washington tomorrow?

HST. I'm making a speech in Topeka first. (*He laughs.*) My mother was a little girl during the Order Number Eleven days down in Cass County. She never forgot that. Every time I went to Kansas, Mama always asked me if I'd run across any of the family silver they stole. (REPORTERS *and* MATT *laugh.*)

FIRST REPORTER. Are you going to recommend a tax increase to Congress? (MATT *clears his throat, concerned, months a silent "no comment" as* HST *looks at him.*)

HST. No. (MATT *looks up in slight disgust.*)

SECOND REPORTER. Then are you going to raise the debt limit? (MATT *bends down, whispers to* HST.)

HST. I certainly am not. (MATT *again looks aloft.*) We will cut public spending.

THIRD REPORTER. On what programs?

HST. The budget boys are studying that now. This government isn't going to spoon-feed anyone not willing to earn an honest living by his own efforts.

FIRST REPORTER. Why is it that Sam Rayburn doesn't move from the Speaker's chair to the House floor to support your proposals? (MATT *bends down, whispers to* HST.)

HST. The Speaker and I are old friends of long standing. But, sometimes Sam gets as stubborn as a mule, and . . . (MATT *clears his throat, taps* HST *on the shoulder.*) uh, no comment. (MATT *sighs, smiles.* REPORTERS *look at him annoyed.*)

SECOND REPORTER. Do you think that Russia will enter the war?

HST. Russia has been in the war for four years.

SECOND REPORTER. I mean against the Japanese.

HST. We're still off the record, aren't we? (REPORTERS *nod, comment affirmatively.*) All right, then. I think, they will. But I'll tell you this. (MATT *listens uneasily, bends closer to hear.*) I'm getting mighty put out with Joe Stalin.

MATT. Uh, Mr. President, I think that . . .

HST. He better get on the ball. I'm tired of baby-sitting the Soviets. (REPORTERS *write furiously*. MATT *throws up his hands*. REPORTERS *cross to chair muttering* "thank you Mr. President," *sit*. HST *follows them amazed*.) Wait a minute! I'm not through! Don't take that without letting me finish.

MATT. (*Resigned, as* HST *crosses to him*.) It's too late.

HST. I had more to say. Why did those guys fly out of here like bats out of hell?

MATT. Read the papers tomorrow and you'll see.

HST. Why, we were off the record.

MATT. You were, but they weren't.

HST. Well, how do you like that! (*Pause*. HST *waves and speaks to fourth wall*.) Hello, Frank. How are you? (*To* MATT.) Ask Bill if there's any lemonade, will you? (MATT *turns, starts to exit, Stage Left, stops as* HST *speaks*.) You know, Matt, sometimes I have trouble remembering that I'm President.

MATT. No comment.

(*BLACKOUT*. HST *and* MATT *cross to chairs, sit*.)

SCENE 6

BILL *rises, crosses to lectern*.

BILL. I was mighty busy that weekend pouring lemonade for everybody who came up to the front porch. It was hot as hell in Independence in the summer, but it's always hot wherever he goes. Back in Washington was no exception.

There was a definite let's-help-Harry attitude during his early days as President. People rallied around him. He was over his head, and he was working hard to do a good job.

But there were many others with a let-Harry-help-himself view. They weren't on his side, and loudly announced that they didn't want to be, like some of

the anti-Truman Republican Congressmen at lunch
one day.

(FOUR CONGRESSMEN *have risen during* BILL'S *lines,
    cross with chairs to Downstage Right Center, sit
    in semi-circle facing fourth wall.* BILL *crosses,
    sits.*)

FIRST CONG. The ship sails on without a captain.
Not that that's any big surprise.

FOURTH CONG. We had an intelligent, informed
President with great charm and appeal in Roosevelt.
What does Truman have?

SECOND CONG. Well, Harry isn't dumb.

THIRD CONG. He isn't? Hell! I sat in the Senate
with him for ten years. What did he ever do there?

FOURTH CONG. The same thing he is doing in the
White House: nothing. We've got a cardboard President, the former Senator from Pendergast.

FIRST CONG. What else do you expect from that
farmer? With him downtown the country is in trouble.
Real trouble. Pass the rolls.

SECOND CONG. Wait a minute. You've got to give
the devil his due. When he was in the Senate, the
Truman Investigating Committee really got our war
effort off the ground. I'll bet it has saved the country
at least fifteen billion dollars, and no telling how many
lives. It probably knocked a year or two off the war.
Who knows where we'd be in this war right now without . . .

FIRST CONG. All right, he's shrewd. Shrewd enough
to create a new committee and make a big fat name
for himself. I'll admit that isn't easy.

FOURTH CONG. The hell it isn't. If Truman did it,
it's bound to be easy. Pass the salt, please.

FIRST CONG. I don't see how the guy got to Washington in the first place. Look at his background. Why, if
he hadn't been a yes man for the Pendergast machine,

he'd be riding a plow in a Missouri cornfield, looking at the ass end of a blind mule. Uh, pardon me.

FIRST CONG. Well, he's gonna be easy to beat in '48. I could beat him myself.

SECOND CONG. Sure you could! I remember right before your last election. You were asking me if I wanted to buy your house in Chevy Chase. (*Others laugh.*)

FOURTH CONG. You gonna vote for him?

SECOND CONG. Go ask that same question to the guy who swings a lunch bucket. He's got a job, so he's got no complaint with the administration.

THIRD CONG. Yeah. But there's a war going on. Where will those jobs be when it's over? Those guys will be walking the streets like in '32. Who's in office? Truman. Who do they blame? Truman.

FOURTH CONG. One term of Harry is all this country will put up with. The people will find out that to err is Truman. (*All laugh.*)

SECOND CONG. That's what we hope. But don't fool yourself that Harry will be an easy opponent. He's scrupulously honest. Every political foe he's ever had agrees to that. He's got a common touch that . . .

FIRST CONG. Common is right.

SECOND CONG. So he didn't go to finishing school. That common touch is what gets him elected.

FOURTH CONG. Huh! Who put him in the White House? The grim reaper!

FIRST CONG. He can't count on that again. That's a tough ticket to get anybody to head up. (*All laugh.*)

SECOND CONG. Harry will get the nomination, and his farm charm will appeal to the little man. Boys, don't think that we've got a Republican shoo-in in '48. It simply ain't gonna be easy.

FOUTH CONG. You talk like Harry.

THIRD CONG. Well, he's got three years to trip over his own feet.

FIRST CONG. Make that "foot." The other one will always be in his mouth.

FOURTH CONG. It's like I heard the other day in the

cloakroom: "I wonder what Truman would do if he was alive . . ." (*All laugh.*)

(*BLACKOUT.* CONGRESSMEN *rise, cross with chairs to their original seating arrangement, sit.*)

SCENE 7

BILL *rises, crosses to lectern.*

BILL. Those were the jokes going around Washington then. You could figure that the Republicans would doom him to failure. But some Democrats, too, remembering FDR, shook their heads. The rest of us hoped, and pulled for the new President who was doing the thing he did best: Admit his shortcomings and work like hell. He'd show 'em! He did, too.

(*BLACKOUT.* BILL *crosses to chair, sits.* MATT *rises, crosses to desk.*)

MATT. Mr. Byrnes said it is urgent that you call him, sir.

HST. It's always urgent with him. Jim's been Secretary of State three weeks, and all he does is call me. Hell with him.

MATT. Sergeant Leonard Cranston is here for the award ceremony. (CRANSTON *rises.*)

HST. Okay. I hope I don't have trouble with it. I'm not very good at these things. Well, send him in, Matt.

MATT. (*Crosses to Downstage Center.*) This way, Sergeant. (CRANSTON *crosses to Center Stage as* HST *rises, crosses to meet him.*) Mr. President, Sergeant Cranston.

(CRANSTON *salutes,* HST *shakes hands with him as greetings are exchanged.* MATT *hands citation to* HST, *which he reads.*)

HST. "For conspicuous heroism and gallantry above and beyond the call of duty at the risk of life, Sergeant Leonard J. Cranston, U. S. Army, did conduct himself with such dedication in action as to inflict serious losses to the enemy. He is herewith recognized and awarded the Congressional Medal of Honor." (HST *hands citation to* MATT, *takes medal from him.*) Sergeant, it is a privilege for me to present you with the nation's highest military award. (*He hangs medal around* CRANSTON'S *neck, shakes his hand.*) I would rather have this medal than be President of the United States.

CRANSTON. Thank you very much, sir. (*He salutes* HST.)

HST. (*Less official, conversationally.*) Well, we're glad that you're home. How do you feel?

CRANSTON. Mr. President, to be honest, I was less nervous in front of a regiment of Germans than I am now. (*All laugh.*)

HST. No need for that. I rode through a lot of French territory when I was in the Field Artillery in 1918. After all, we Army men stick together.

CRANSTON. That's right, sir. We do.

HST. I suppose you're on furlough, Sergeant.

CRANSTON. Yes, sir. Three weeks.

HST. Well, I hope you enjoy it. The whole country owes you a great debt of gratitude.

CRANSTON. Thank you, sir. (*He salutes, does an about face, crosses to chair, sits.*)

MATT. Now that wasn't too difficult, was it, Mr. President?

HST. It's a big moment for me, but I still never know what to say. That business about us old Army men is a lot of baloney for a serious occasion like that.

MATT. To coin your phrase, it rang the bell. You made him feel at ease.

HST. At least it was better than the last time. I

can hardly hold my voice steady whenever I give a medal to a widow or a father. What an old fool I am!

(MATT *and* HST *cross Upstage, as* MATT *puts his hand on* HST's *shoulder.* MATT *sits at desk,* HST *sits on Downstage Right corner of desk, picks up Kansas City "Star," reads.* BESS *rises, crosses to desk, carrying appointment book.*)

BESS. Harry, do you have a minute to talk?

HST. (*Putting down paper.*) Sure, Bess. I was just checking what's going on at home. (*He looks at her.*) Say, haven't we met before?

BESS. From the little time I get to see you, I'm not surprised you ask.

HST. Do you have an appointment?

BESS. All right, now.

HST. Honey, we'll take a minute. (*He rises.*) Anything the matter?

BESS. What do we have scheduled this week?

HST. (*Checking appointment book from desk.*) Tonight is the benefit at Constitution Hall for Navy Relief. And tomorrow is the reception for the new Swedish Ambassador.

BESS. Another state occasion. Do we have to go to that?

HST. It's important, honey. Besides, you like Swedish meat balls.

BESS. (*Crosses to Downstage Right Center.*) Standing around in a smoky room where you can't hear a thing because everybody talks at the same time. (*She turns, faces* HST.) In eight languages.

HST. I'll talk to you. In Missouri-ish.

BESS. After an hour, my feet hurt so bad I can't believe it.

HST. One of the hazards of being First Lady. (*He crosses to* BESS, *takes her hand.*) Just because you're nice, I'll let you go barefoot.

BESS. I wish I could. What's on for Wednesday?

HST. A dinner party at the George Allens.

BESS. Not the Allens.

HST. They don't bite.

BESS. No. I just don't happen to care for George's jokes. What about Thursday?

HST. (*Crosses to desk, looks at book.*) Let's see. On Thursday we go to a dedication of some thing. (*He studies his book.*) I can't read it here.

BESS. Can't we finesse that one, and stay home? You are going at such a pace that I'm worried.

HST. About me? Huh! (*He pats midsection, flexes muscles.*) Healthy as a horse. Wally Graham says so every day when he comes here.

BESS. You work so hard, though. All day, then bring papers upstairs until eleven.

HST. You haven't known me when I didn't. Farming never was easy, if you recall.

BESS. You look tired. (*She crosses to him, puts hand on his shoulder.*) Harry, how long has it been since we had a night alone when you could relax without a crowd of people saying "yes, Mr. President, no, Mr. President"?

HST. Didn't we know what we were in for the day we moved into the taxpayer's house?

BESS. If I had, I'd have never let you be drafted by Roosevelt. When you were Senator, we knew where we'd be nearly every night: our apartment at 4701 Connecticut Avenue.

HST. And you were getting bored with me.

BESS. I was not! I had you all to myself and I liked it!

HST. (*Puts his arm around her.*) I'm kidding, honey.

BESS. Promise me one thing.

HST. (*Drops arm around BESS.*) What?

BESS. That you won't run in '48, and we can go home instead of living in this goldfish bowl.

HST. Bess, it's not all that bad. (*Takes several steps*

to Left.) Your bridge club from home spends next week with us. Think of all the money you'll win— maybe five dollars. Besides, you always said you liked Washington. (*He crosses Upstage, sits on desk.*)

BESS. I do, but it's not Independence.

HST. The rent is right.

BESS. Please, Harry.

HST. Now, what else is bothering you? It isn't Mama's visit, is it?

BESS. Of course not. It's Margaret.

HST. Margie? The only thing I'm concerned about is that she's never learned to swim.

BESS. Well, I wish that was all that worried me.

HST. That girl's all right. She's got her musical career, and it's going to be a good career too, if I'm any judge.

BESS. Look at her social life. How would you like it if some secret service man had followed us around when we were dating?

HST. John Dorsey is an improvement over what I had to contend with.

BESS. What do you mean?

HST. Why, your mother thought she was Sherlock Holmes.

BESS. Be serious. Margaret and Drucie Snyder spent a whole evening last week with their beaux trying to ditch that man.

HST. If they had, I'd have fired him.

BESS. But what if she had? Why, anything could have happened. Somebody could have kidnapped her.

HST. At least she could have gotten some privacy that way.

BESS. Harry, how can you make light of this?

HST. Honey, I'm not. (*He crosses, puts arm around* BESS.) There are several nice young men who take her out. Even a couple of Republicans.

BESS. (*Crosses to Downstage Right Center.*) If any-one ever proposed to her, Dorsey would probably interrupt with "what do you have to say to that, Miss Truman." (*Crosses Upstage to Right desk chair, sits.*) It's no way to be courted.

HST. She said she'd never get engaged while we were here. I know how she can handle Dorsey, Bess.

BESS. How?

HST. The next time she and whatshisname get close, she can say to Dorsey: "I've got the President's permission. It's all right if he kisses me." (*He laughs; BESS doesn't.*)

BESS. If you were in her shoes, you wouldn't laugh about it. It would help, too, if you'd remember who her escorts are and not refer to them as "Whatshisname."

HST. Okay, I'll try. I'll tell you something else: We'll skip the dedication and plan a state occasion for just the two of us, and I'll hand in my resignation. Will that make you happy? (HST *takes her hand.* BESS *smiles;* HST *frowns.*) Only one thing. A President never resigned before. Do I send it to the presiding officer of the Senate, to Chief Justice Fred Vinson, or to whom it may concern?

BESS. Just give it to me. I'll get it in the right hands, and have you packed the same day.

HST. Now Boss, if you'll excuse me, I've got to run the country. (BESS *and* HST *rise, he kisses her on the cheek as* MATT *rises, crosses to desk.*)

MATT. Mr. Presi . . . oh. I beg your pardon.

HST. It's all right, Matt. She's my wife. (BESS *smiles, pats* HST *on the arm, crosses to chair, sits.*)

MATT. Are you ready for the press conference? (RE-PORTERS *rise, cross to Downstage Right, confer.*)

HST. Time for that already?

MATT. Yes, sir. If you'll pardon a prediction, I think you're going to play second fiddle today.

HST. No bet. Mama will have the limelight, all right. What do you think they'll ask her.

MATT. Oh, about how she likes having you in the White House, I suppose.

HST. I just heard one female's comments on that.

MATT. Do you want to talk to her first?

HST. Yes. Give us just a minute. (MRS. TRUMAN *rises, crosses, as HST crosses to her, kisses her.*) Morning, Mama. How did you sleep?

MRS. TRUMAN. All right for a strange place, Harry.

HST. (*Puts left arm around her, leads her to Downstage Left Center.*) That's not a very nice thing to say about the White House. (MATT *crosses to Left of* REPORTERS.)

MRS. TRUMAN. I can't get used to all these servants running around.

HST. Just remember that you don't need to make your own bed.

MRS. TRUMAN. Too late. I already did. (REPORTERS *cross to Center Stage with notebooks.*)

MATT. Ladies and gentlemen, the President of the United States.

HST. And his mother.

FIRST REPORTER. Could we ask some questions of Mrs. Truman?

HST. Mama, could they?

MRS. TRUMAN. Well, I don't know . . .

SECOND REPORTER. Mrs. Truman, do you like Washington?

MRS. TRUMAN. Yes, but I miss my own home in Missouri.

THIRD REPORTER. How long do you plan to stay?

MRS. TRUMAN. Oh, another day or two, if I don't wear out my welcome first. (*She starts to cross toward Stage Left.* HST *takes her arm, restrains her.*) Well, excuse me now . . .

FIRST REPORTER. Have you heard that one of the bedrooms is haunted, and a former President comes back at night?

Mrs. Truman. If he does, he'll be just as scared of me as I am of him.

Second Reporter. What have you been doing in Washington?

Mrs. Truman. Oh, helping out a little.

Third Reporter. You mean with the government?

Mrs. Truman. No. I've done some mending and things for Bess, and we went for a ride yesterday. Well, I ought to go along and not waste your time.

First Reporter. Just one more question, please, Mrs. Truman. You must be very proud that a son of yours is in the White House. (*Pause.*)

Mrs. Truman. Well, yes, but I have another son who lives down the road a piece from me, and I'm just as proud of him.

Second Reporter. We'd like a picture, Mrs. Truman. (Reporters *cross closer to her, pantomime taking pictures.* Third Reporter *crosses Downstage of her with his back to the fourth wall.*) Now if you'd stand a little closer to your mother, Mr. President.

Third Reporter. Over here, Mrs. Truman. A little more to the right. (Mrs. Truman *takes several confused steps.*)

HST. Boys, around here *I* decide if we move to the right. (HST *and* Reporters *laugh.*)

First Reporter. Now smile please. Thank you.

Second Reporter. Just one more. Mrs. Truman, if you'd move just a little, and . . .

Mrs. Truman. Fiddlesticks! Harry, why didn't you tell me about this, and I would have stayed at home. (*She crosses to chair, sits.* Reporters, *except for* Third, *cross to Stage Right.*)

Reporters. Thank you, Mrs. Truman. Thank you, Mr. President.

Third Reporter. I'd like to ask one question, Mr. President.

Matt. I'm sorry, but . . .

HST. So far this press conference hasn't been too

tiring on me. If you want to ask some impudent questions, I'll give you some impudent answers.

THIRD REPORTER. What is the new agreement with Russia?

HST. What agreement?

THIRD REPORTER. Secretary of State Byrnes mentioned it at his press conference this morning. (MATT *clears his throat;* HST *looks at him, speaks positively.*)

HST. There is no further statement on it at this time.

REPORTERS. Thank you, Mr. President. (REPORTERS *cross to chairs, sit.*)

HST. (*Mad.*) Matt, get Byrnes over here, *now!*

MATT. He's here with the other Cabinet members for their meeting.

HST. Send him in. Privately.

MATT. Yes, sir. (*He crosses to desk, sits.*)

HST. It's time I spoke to him in the same restrained manner that a sergeant speaks to a mule.

(HST *crosses to desk, sits. Secretary of State* JAMES
F. BYRNES *rises, crosses to desk. His attitude is patient intolerance.*)

BYRNES. Hello, Harry. (*He sits in Right desk chair.*) You look as if your vacation at Key West agreed with . . .

HST. Why the hell wasn't I notified about your press conference?

BYRNES. I didn't know you wanted to be.

HST. You know the rule.

BYRNES. What rule?

HST. The damn standing rule on clearing press conferences through the White House. You didn't do it.

BYRNES. You were out of town.

HST. You think we don't have telephones in Independence?

BYRNES. I don't know what you have in Independence.

HST. Don't give me that, Byrnes.

BYRNES. Harry, when you give me authority, I take it.

HST. Then find out what it includes. You told them about some damn agreement with the Russians.

BYRNES. They're our allies.

HST. That doesn't mean we broadcast every security move we make with the Soviets. Maybe you don't know it, but there's a war going on.

BYRNES. Maybe you don't either.

HST. I don't need your petty insolence, Jim. (*He rises.*) Do you like being my secretary of state?

BYRNES. Do you want to fire me?

HST. No. But only because you've got talent. If you won't cooperate, then Dean Acheson puts his stuff in your desk.

BYRNES. The minute he does, you know what happens to our foreign policy.

HST. I make the foreign policy and it doesn't include appeasement. All I want you to do is carry it out. Is that clear?

BYRNES. It's very clear that you think you can run the entire government. (*He rises.*) The rest of us are pawns. (*He leans on desk.*) Harry, don't kid yourself into thinking you're a Roosevelt.

HST. You've been like the little boy who took his ball and went home because he didn't get to bat. (*He leans on desk, eye to eye with* BYRNES.) The next time you do, South Carolina can have you for keeps. You were FDR's fair-haired boy. We don't have those around any more.

BYRNES. You need all of them you can get.

HST. You're still mad because I got the nomination in '44 when you thought you had it in the bag.

BYRNES. That was almost enough to make a good loyal Democrat turn Republican.

HST. (*He speaks with controlled anger.*) That's all, Mr. Secretary.

(BYRNES *crosses to chair, sits.* HST *sits.* BLACK-OUT.)

SCENE 8

BILL *rises, crosses to lectern.* MARSHALL *crosses to desk, looks over* HST's *right shoulder at newspaper he is reading.*

BILL. Yes sir, the President sure got mad at his secretary of state. But it didn't compare with the fireworks that went off a few days later. (BILL, *carrying newspaper, crosses Upstage to desk.*)

MARSHALL. I can't understand how he could write this.

HST. That no-good son of a . . .

BILL. Hello, General Marshall. Here is your paper, Mr. President.

HST. (*Snaps.*) I've seen it! (*Throws paper on floor.*)

BILL. Oh.

HST. Go find Mrs. Truman! (BILL *turns, picks up paper quickly, frightened.*) And send in Rose Conway!

BILL. Yes, sir. (*He crosses quickly to chair, sits.*)

HST. I'll bet he wasn't even there. He doesn't know a sharp from a flat, or his . . .

MARSHALL. I considered him a good critic until now.

HST. I never did. This proves it. (BESS *rises, crosses to desk.* HST *rises.*) Did you see this?

BESS. Yes, I saw it.

HST. That's the worst thing I ever read. (HST *crosses Downstage, paces through the rest of the Scene, speaks loudly.*) Believe me, I know music, and that guy is dead wrong. Dead wrong!

BESS. Harry, there isn't any point in getting so riled up. (BESS *crosses several steps Downstage toward* HST.) You're taking it worse than Margaret.

HST. It's obvious he did it because she's my daughter. The offspring of the President have no special privileges. They shouldn't have any special liabilities either.

MARSHALL. The only thing he didn't criticize was the varnish on the piano.

HST. Yeah. That "Post" critic put my baby as low as he could and made her accompanist look like a dub. He's got to be tone deaf.

BESS. Now, Harry . . .

HST. I'm going to fix his wagon. (ROSE *rises, crosses to desk.*) Rose, we're going to write a letter you'll have to put on asbestos.

ROSE. Sir?

MARSHALL. (*Crosses Downstage to* HST.) Mr. President, you might wait twenty-four hours to think it through.

HST. I'm not going to wait ten minutes! (MARSHALL *crosses Upstage to* BESS; *both gesture the futility of the situation.*) He'll learn what I think of him. All right, Rose, write this to that stupid critic. (HST *paces, almost shouting.*) "Your review sounded like it was written by an eight-ulcer man on a four-ulcer job, and all four ulcers working. I never met you, but if I do, you'll need a new nose and plenty of beefsteak."

(*BLACKOUT. The four Downstage-most Right actors rise, strike chairs to Right wings, exit, remain Offstage until Act Two.*)

SCENE 9

BILL *rises, crosses to lectern, speaks with almost humorous touch.*

BILL. The, uh, *private* letter soon was public property. In twelve hours, you read it in any paper you picked up. As the old man said, sometimes he forgot that he was President. (BILL *becomes serious.*) But he had a lot more to worry about than that critic, something he hadn't been able to forget about for one minute. (BILL *speaks loudly and angrily.*)

Put yourself in his shoes. Put the monkey on your back. It's up to you—and only you—to decide. There's a war going on. A couple of million men in the Pacific are getting shot at for a living. Some career. Every day somebody gets a wire from you that says their boy isn't coming home again, and they hang a gold star in the window. You've got to end the war. There's a way to do it, quick. (*Pause, then more intent and louder.*) What are you going to do? Now! Hurry up! Decide! They're killing your neighbor's boy on some damn island! End the war! Kill all those Jap women! They're enemies, too! You can't help it! It won't be your fault! (*Pause; then a quiet question.*) Will it? (BILL *crosses to Upstage Right, carrying eight note pads, which he gives to each character on their Downstage side as he mentions their names.*)

That was July 20, 1945. There was a lot of big brass— (*All actors seated at Stage Right rise, bring chairs toward Center Stage inside sight lines if necessary.*) in the Cabinet Room that morning: Secretary Stimson, General Marshall, Admiral Leahy, Admiral King, General Arnold, Doctor Conant, Doctor Compton, and Doctor . . . (BILL *pauses.*) I don't seem to recollect your name, sir, but here's a note pad for you. (BILL *exits, Downstage Right. HST brings Right desk chair over to sit at the head of the imaginary table, all sit.*)

STIMSON. The test of the atomic bomb in New Mexico was conclusive. (*All comment affirmatively.*)

HST. I have heard that good news. Then the bomb will do what it should?

STIMSON. Yes. The test bomb had the force of twenty thousand tons of TNT.

CONANT. To put it in unscientific terms, Mr. President, it blew the most hellacious hole you ever saw. (*Restrained laughter.*)

COMPTON. Jim, may I explain?

CONANT. Go ahead, Karl.

COMPTON. (*Rises.*) Had our test been over a populated area, a Japanese city, there would have been total destruction for two miles from ground zero. Damage would have reached out to four or five miles. Those it didn't kill would have been seriously injured and burned from the intense heat and power of the blast.

HST. How do you know this? Were any of your project people injured?

COMPTON. Yes, sir. A cook was blinded. He didn't have protective glasses and looked directly at the blast in spite of urgent warnings. Light from it was seen in El Paso, 180 miles away.

CONANT. Used in quantity, Mr. President, atomic warfare could destroy all life on earth.

HST. Do you know yet exactly how this affects the human system?

COMPTON. We're fairly sure. Radioactive particles on the skin can cause death. In a lesser amount, they destroy certain body functions. An unknown factor, and perhaps the most serious of all, is that these rays can get into food which might endanger future generations by some sort of genetic deterioration.

HST. We have got to outlaw war. It is either that, or perish. The next one, God forbid, with this kind of force available, would make Hell look like a playground.

MARSHALL. We have repeatedly asked Japan to surrender.

HST. Yes. They have ignored the millions of leaflets we have dropped telling them to surrender or face destruction. But I had no idea that complete destruction meant levelling their country.

COMPTON. One bomb won't do that, Mr. President.

HST. But it will destroy everything for miles. We haven't told them about our A-bomb. Could we meet with the Japanese brass, say, in the Pacific, aboard a ship, and drop another atom bomb on some little atoll? If they saw this weapon, they'd change their tune and surrender.

CONANT. Yes, we could. However, bear in mind, Mr. President, that the chances of this bomb working are no better than half.

HST. Okay. Suppose we drop it, to show that we mean business. It's a dud. Then we drop the other one.

COMPTON. One fails, one works. That's the end of our arsenal. We've only got two.

HST. If the first one works, we've got one left. The Japanese either surrender then, or we drop the second one down their throats.

CONANT. What if it doesn't detonate?

HST. Hm. Then we're in trouble. (*He rises, takes several steps to Left.*) How long before we've got another bomb ready to go? A month?

COMPTON. Maybe six months.

MARSHALL. That means six more months of war.

ARNOLD. Mr. President, do our allies know we have this weapon?

HST. Yes. Churchill and I discussed it at length at Potsdam. He favors it. If we use it, and I repeat, *if,* what targets do you recommend? (*He sits.*)

MARSHALL. Out of eleven proposed cities, we are of the opinion that Hiroshima should be the initial target.

HST. Why?

MARSHALL. It is an Army center and a military supply port. The second most critical target is Nagasaki.

HST. Do you all agree? (KING *and* ARNOLD *comment in the affirmative.* LEAHY *rises, speaks positively.*)

LEAHY. Very definitely not.

HST. Why not, Bill?

LEAHY. We have seen one demonstration that a
bunch of physicists experimented with. Now they tell
us that a second bomb might not go off. I'd hate like
hell to rely on . . .

CONANT. Yes, Admiral Leahy, but its chances of
detonating are equally as good.

HST. Let him finish, please.

LEAHY. We don't know what this thing can do. We
do know what conventional bombs and naval gunfire
do because they fire every day. (*Sits, satisfied.*)

COMPTON. The power of one A-bomb is equal to
20,000 tons of TNT.

LEAHY. Ours go off every time. On a precise target.
That's reliable weaponry. We could be making a grave
error to depend on this scientific toy. It is a two billion
dollar professor's dream.

HST. Bill, we still have our other weapons if it
doesn't work.

LEAHY. The damn thing won't work. And I speak
as an ordinance officer with a Navy career behind me.
I am against this gamble, and urge you to press on and
invade Japan.

MARSHALL. If I may say something, Mr. President.

HST. Shoot.

MARSHALL. This new weapon staggers the imagina-
tion. It is bigger than the total tonnage of explosives
expended to date. It is thoroughly desirable toward
ending the war, while being disastrous in the cost of
human life.

SCIENTIST. (*Leaning forward, raising his hand. He
gets louder through this Scene, finally reaching a
frenzied and hysterical pitch.*) Mr. President?

HST. Yes, Doctor?

SCIENTIST. There is another side to this.

HST. I want to hear every side.

SCIENTIST. Are you aware what the toll of this
weapon would be?

HST. General Marshall has stated it privately to me. (*To* MARSHALL.) Would you go over it again, George?

MARSHALL. We are planning an invasion of Japan this year. Our casualties are estimated at 250,000 Americans killed, and 500,000 more wounded. The Japanese will make a fanatical last-ditch defense, costing them several million dead.

SCIENTIST. That's just a prediction.

MARSHALL. Of course. We haven't tried it. If we use the A-bomb, it is thought that the dead will number 100,000 in each target area, in addition to the probability of 200,000 wounded.

SCIENTIST. Maimed, General? (*He rises.*) Blinded? Crippled?

MARSHALL. All right—maimed, blinded, crippled, whatever you . . .

SCIENTIST. Or the harm to future generations?

MARSHALL. As an expert you'd agree that any estimate is almost impossible.

SCIENTIST. I would. But you'd agree that quite a large number of innocent Japanese would suffer.

MARSHALL. True, but I am trying to point out, Doctor, that to use these bombs, will save a quarter of a million American lives, and shorten the war by six months to a year.

SCIENTIST. That is *your* prediction.

MARSHALL. It is a considered calculated military prediction, and not mine alone.

SCIENTIST. As against certain immediate annihilation of 200,000 Japanese—innocent civilians, women, children. (*He crosses to Left of* HST.)

MARSHALL. You forget that many are war industry workers who make the weapons that are killing our troops this minute.

SCIENTIST. Mr. President, an American victory is our only goal. It is now in sight. This mass slaughter of civilians is unnecessary. Many of us who worked on

atomic fission are against its use for warfare. We were
led to believe that it was to be used for industrial
power and ship propulsion, not as a weapon directly
against human beings. We know what it can do.

COMPTON. Many of us favor it. (*He rises.*) I'd like
to add, Mr. President . . .

SCIENTIST. Had we thought that the Manhattan
Project meant genocide for defenseless people, and
that . . .

COMPTON. (*Louder.*) Let me finish.

SCIENTIST. . . . It would be used for death, we
would have been conscientious objectors like others
who won't bear arms. We were betrayed when we
weren't informed that this was to kill, to destroy
lives . . .

COMPTON. (*Angry.*) Will you let me finish?

HST. One at a time, please. I want to hear everybody and I can't do it when you both are talking. Dr.
Compton.

COMPTON. (*Quietly, as* SCIENTIST *turns, crosses
several steps toward Downstage Left.*) I started to
say that the majority of us urge, with full knowledge
of the consequences, that you make all haste to use it
against the enemy.

SCIENTIST. It is unthinkable that we, whose only
cause has been to put down an aggressor, can become
aggressors ourselves and kill the innocent. To use force
on those who bear arms is one thing. To kill a child is
another. (*He crosses several steps to Stage Left.*)

HST. Let me make this clear, Doctor. I don't hunt,
because I do not believe in shooting anything that
cannot shoot back.

SCIENTIST. (*Turns, points at* HST, *crosses quickly to
him.*) You are about to! You are getting ready to!

HST. I am opposed to any kind of killing, whether
by atomic bomb or bow and arrow. We are engaged in
war. Harry Truman's opinion is not of importance.
The decision by the President of the United States is.
The buck stops here.

SCIENTIST. I have pointed out that killing of masses of Japanese civilians who cannot shoot back is a moral wrong. It cannot be condoned by anyone who calls himself a Christian.

MARSHALL. Mr. President?

HST. General.

MARSHALL. No one abhors killing of the innocent more than a professional soldier. Yet we . . .

SCIENTIST. Are those Japanese children who will die from this bomb attacking us?

MARSHALL. Our oath is, and will continue to be . . .

SCIENTIST. (*Loud, intense.*) Are they, General? Are those little slant-eyed kids taking a shot at our soldiers? Are they? What have they done? Answer me!

HST. Please, Doctor.

SCIENTIST. Nothing! That's what they've done! You want to kill them! Snuff out their lives like that! (*He snaps fingers.*) Or worse, have them suffer in a lingering and painful death from radiation.

HST. Doctor, if you can't speak in a rational manner, I'm going to ask you to leave.

SCIENTIST. I will! But not without telling you that you are traitors! Traitors to the human race! You care nothing for lives! (*He crosses several steps Downstage, points to* COMPTON *and* CONANT.) You want to see if your precious experiment, your equation, this plaything of yours, will work. (*He crosses several steps Upstage, points to* KING, ARNOLD, LEAHY, *and* MARSHALL.) You are professional killers! You get paid for how many people lie dead! (*He crosses several steps Upstage to* HST, *points at him.*) You! I pity you if you murder, I said murder, those Japanese! The blood is on your hands! Harry Truman, President or not, can never escape answering your God for this crime of genocide. If you kill with this bomb, I hope you rot in hell! (SCIENTIST, *who is almost sobbing, crosses to chair, faces fourth wall with his head in his hands as all watch him. There is a pause.* HST *rises, slowly, crosses slowly several steps toward Downstage Center*

*as all watch him. He stops, looks to Left wings,
crosses to Right several steps, stops, speaks quietly but
positively.)*

HST. We use the bomb. (SCIENTIST *shakes his head
as all others lean back, nod heads in relieved agreement. HST crosses to Downstage Center. He folds his
hands, closes his eyes, raises his head, and prays.)* Oh,
Almighty God, help me to be, to think, to do what is
right, because it is right . . .

(*BLACKOUT, as* HST *remains at Downstage
Center.*)

SCENE 10

BILL *enters, Stage left, crosses to lectern, speaks in
quiet, factual, unemotional voice.*

BILL. On August 5th, the Enola Gay dropped an
atomic bomb on Hiroshima. On August 7th, a second
A-bomb was dropped on Nagasaki. On August 14,
1945, Japan surrendered. (BILL *sees* HST *at Downstage Center, crosses to him quickly, speaks excitedly
to the tired, quiet, almost distant* HST.) Mr. President!
Mr. President! Peace! At last! What a great day!

HST. (*Solemn.*) Yes, it is, Bill.

BILL. The war is over! It's wonderful!

HST. Now to make this an honorable and lasting
peace.

BILL. (*Conversationally, with genuine feeling.*)
You've been a great leader, Mr. President. You de-
serve all the credit for our victory. (*He looks at* HST,
concerned.) Are you all right, sir?

HST. Yes, I'm all right. I can't help wondering,
though. (*He crosses slowly and aimlessly to Stage
Right.* BILL *continues to look at him questioningly.*
HST *looks at note in his hand, reads.*) "Hiroshima

casualty estimates: 78,000 people killed, 150,000 wounded, 99% of all buildings demolished." (HST *wads up note, drops it, speaks to himself, facing fourth wall, as slow curtain starts.*) 78,000 killed, 150,000 wounded. I can't help wondering . . .

CURTAIN—END OF ACT ONE

ACT TWO

Scene 11

SCENE: *The Stage is set as in Act One, with all actors in their chairs, including the four at Downstage Right who were absent in Scenes 9 and 10. The sole exception is that* MAMA TRUMAN *is not present in this act and her chair has been struck.*

TIME: *At present.*

AT RISE: BILL *rises, crosses to lectern, speaks in a happy and excited voice.*

BILL. The war was over. Hallelujah! Millions of men came home and we all rejoiced. It was a great time. (*He speaks more seriously.*) But the President's problems went right along in our change from war to peace. He tried to solve them in his usual work day: from five A.M. to eleven o'clock, and no time-and-a-half. If people were talking about pay raises, he didn't get one. He was too busy worrying about other things. (*He picks up paper, reads.*) Like the Kansas City "Star" says here in May, 1946: Railroad Unions Threaten Strike. (*He crosses to chair, sits.* MATT *rises, crosses to desk.*)

MATT. Mr. Whitney and Mr. Johnston are here, Mr. President. (WHITNEY *and* JOHNSTON *rise.*)

HST. Aren't they always? Well, bring them in, Matt.

MATT. (*To* WHITNEY *and* JOHNSTON.) This way, gentlemen.

(MATT *crosses to chair, sits.* WHITNEY *and* JOHNSTON *cross to desk.* WHITNEY *extends his hand, which* HST *declines.*)

48

WHITNEY. Mr. Presi . . .

HST. Have a seat. (WHITNEY *and* JOHNSTON *sit by desk.*) I said I'd see you if you had something new. Let's hear it.

WHITNEY. Our union has made a real attempt to be equitable. With rail profits up like they are . . .

HST. Would the railroads still have this level of profit if the new peacetime boom fades?

JOHNSTON. Our studies here prove they would.

HST. You obviously haven't read theirs.

JOHNSTON. Oh, yes we have, Mr. President.

HST. Boys, everybody agreed that your unions are entitled to more money. But Al, you're asking for the moon. Take the offer and let's settle this.

JOHNSTON. Harry, we don't want to do what John L. Lewis' miners did.

HST. You said you had new information. (*He looks at his watch.*) So far, I haven't heard it.

WHITNEY. (*Direct, level.*) You haven't forgotten that labor backed your nomination in '44, have you?

HST. Now you're saying that labor knew I'd be fair, so I owe them this inflationary increase? (*Mad.*) That kind of talk hints at blackmail, and I don't like it!

WHITNEY. I thought I was a better friend of yours than this, Harry.

HST. You are. Take a cruise with me down the Potomac aboard the "Williamsburg." That's what I do for my friends. But I'm not about to wreck the economy for a friendship.

JOHNSTON. You remember your other friends when it comes to favors and appointments.

HST. Every single one of my appointments has been to competent people. Friends? Hell, yes. Did you ever know anyone who appointed his enemies?

WHITNEY. Including John Snyder—from Missouri, incidentally—as Secretary of the Treasury?

HST. Including John Snyder. (*He rises.*) Get this

straight, Whitney. My people do a job, or I fire them
if they get too big for their breeches. Ask Henry
Wallace. Now . . . (*He crosses several steps toward
Stage Left.*) my emergency board recommended $1.28
and hour raise. You are asking for a ridiculous $2.20.
I'm going to support my board. Do you want it?

JOHNSTON. (*Rises, crosses several steps Downstage,
irritated, speaks over his shoulder.*) I'm sorry, Mr.
President.

WHITNEY. I can't accept, either. (*He rises.*) We'll
advise our members that you leave us with no option.

HST. Then I'll tell the country that what you are
demanding is a hell of a way to run a railroad! I
represent 150 million Americans. (*He sits, takes pen,
signs paper.*) Strike, and the government runs the
trains.

JOHNSTON. The Congress won't pass that bill you
signed there to give you the power.

WHITNEY. It's political suicide, Harry, and you
know it.

HST. I'm not a candidate for anything. I ran the
street cars here in Washington when nobody thought
I would. When you walk out that door, Whitney, I'm
going to be the chief conductor, just like this bill says.
You can put that in your pipe and smoke it! (WHITNEY
and JOHNSTON *cross to chairs, mad, sit.* MATT *rises,
watches* WHITNEY *and* JOHNSTON *cross, crosses to desk,
speaks solicitously.*)

MATT. Are you all right, Mr. President?

HST. (*Terse.*) Hell yes I'm all right!

MATT. Those two aren't. That's the only reason I
asked. What did you do to them?

HST. (*Rises, writes on notepad, crosses to Downstage Center.*) Call Ken McKellar. I'm making a
speech at a joint session tomorrow.

MATT. That's the stiffest piece of legislation any
President has ever wanted. You know what Senator
Pepper said.

HST. That I'd be called a dictator? He knows better. I don't say this is smart politically. It's necessary, that's all. Matt, you worry more than Bess.

MATT. (*With a futile shrug, crosses to desk, sits.*) Somebody needs to.

(*BLACKOUT, as* HST *stands Downstage Center.*)

SCENE 12

BILL *rises, crosses to lectern.*

BILL. The House and Senate listened when he told them how to run a railroad, too. (*He crosses to chair, sits.* HST *crosses to lectern.*)

HST. What we are dealing with here is not labor as a whole. We are dealing with a handful of men who are striking against their own government and against every one of their fellow citizens.

I therefore request strong emergency legislation to authorize injunctive proceedings against any union leader who persists in striking against the government. I hope that you will authorize the President to draft into the armed forces all workers who strike.

(*Secretary of the Senate* J. LESLIE BIFFLE *rises, crosses to* HST, *hands him a note.*)

BIFFLE. Excuse me, Mr. President. I've got an important message for you. (*He crosses to chair, sits.* HST *reads note, speaks in a relieved and happier voice.*)

HST. I am happy to announce that the railroad strike has been settled on terms previously accepted by all except the two unions.

(*BLACKOUT.* HST *crosses to desk, sits.*)

SCENE 13

BILL *rises, crosses to lectern.*

BILL. So they called him the nation's number-one strike-breaker. The trains kept running, didn't they? He was a hell of an engineer.

He settled one domestic issue, and went immediately into another. He got some mighty high-priced help on it, too. It isn't often that Washington has two Presidents. But it did when President Truman got President Hoover to come back to work. Ever wonder what one President says to another? (*He crosses to chair, sits. HST, seated at desk, speaks into phone.*)

HST. Morning, Mr. President. This is Harry Truman . . . I'm fine. How are you? . . . Good. I want to thank you for the excellent job your Hoover Commission did . . . Well, I guess all of us old fire horses are alike: when the bell rings, we go . . . (*He laughs.*) The thing that amazed me was to see a Republican do such a good job . . . Drop in at your old house before you leave . . . Goodbye. (*He hangs up phone, becomes distant and serious as he looks off toward Downstage Right. There is a slight pause. MATT rises, crosses to desk.*)

MATT. Mr. President. (*Pause.*) Mr. President?

HST. (*Faces MATT.*) Yes? What is it, Matt?

MATT. I want to extend my sympathy on your mother's death, sir.

HST. Thank you, Matt. I'm sure going to miss her. Mama and I were very close.

MATT. (*With kindly humor.*) I'll never forget her comment after you were sworn in as Vice President. She said, "Now, Harry, you behave yourself."

HST. (*Smiles.*) Yes, she had a great sense of humor.

(*BLACKOUT. MATT crosses to desk, sits.*)

Scene 14

BILL *rises, crosses to lectern.*

BILL. No matter what, business in the White House had to go on. Dealing with Presidents, Prime Ministers, Senators—all kinds of Senators. (*He crosses to chairs, sits.* MATT *rises, crosses to desk.*)

MATT. Clark Griffith of the baseball team to see you, sir. (*He crosses to desk, sits.* GRIFFITH *rises, crosses to desk.* HST *rises, points to him.*)

HST. Just because I didn't make spring training doesn't mean I'm not ready to play. Now get this: with the score tied in the last of the ninth, the bases loaded, and your clean-up man at bat, what do you do?

GRIFFITH. Hm. Since that's as close as we've been to winning all year, I'd expect to see dancing in the streets. (GRIFFITH *shakes hands with* HST.) Good morning, Mr. President.

HST. Sit down, Griff. You're lucky that you've only got Senator trouble. I have to worry about the House, too. So far my batting average there looks like Jake Early's. (*They laugh.* HST *crosses Downstage of desk, faces fourth wall, swings an imaginary bat left-handed.*) Could you use a Texas-league hitter?

GRIFFITH. Give you $200,000.

HST. (*Waves his hand.*) Couldn't take a cut in pay like that.

GRIFFITH. What's your position?

HST. Behind the plate. With all the hell the Republicans throw at me, catching Dutch Leonard would be a breeze.

GRIFFITH. (*He laughs, takes baseball from pocket, gives it to* HST.) Here's the ball you threw out at our opening game.

HST. Thanks, Griff. That's the last time I was there. Who do you play tonight?

GRIFFITH. New York. Your box is waiting. Can you make it?

HST. A Missourian to see the Yankees? Not a chance! All my southern ancestors would come back to haunt me. (HST *sits on desk.*) I'd rather be there, than at the dinner we're having for some ambassador or other. You've really got a good job. You get to see baseball every day.

GRIFFITH. Sometimes I'm not sure it's baseball. (*He takes another ball from pocket, gives it to* HST.) Mr. President, if you'd be so kind . . .

HST. Another ball for me? Ain't that somepin!

GRIFFITH. Well, not exactly. The club wants you to autograph it for our trophy case.

HST. You Senators are all alike. First you give, then you take away. (*Both laugh, as* HST *autographs ball, tosses it to* GRIFFITH.) Tell them that this goes with my prediction of a World Series in Griffith Stadium this October.

GRIFFITH. If we're still in the majors then, I'll be happy. You know the old story: Washington—first in war, first in peace, and last in the American League.

(*BLACKOUT.* GRIFFITH *and* HST *cross to chairs, sit.*)

SCENE 15

BILL *rises, crosses to lectern.*

BILL. There were still those Senators to deal with on The Hill. Some of the most difficult were in his own Party, too. This was Election Year—1948. (*He crosses to chair, sits.* SENATORS *rise, bring chairs to Downstage Right Center in a semi-circle, sit, face fourth wall.*)

FIRST SEN. I tell you we've got no choice. We've got to go with him.

SECOND SEN. For certain defeat? Don't be naive.

THIRD SEN. It's either back him, or admit that our Democratic administration hasn't been a good one.

SECOND SEN. When we're in the White House, that makes it good, at least as far as we're concerned. But ask the man on the street.

FOURTH SEN. Then go ask his wife. She knows what happened to the cost of living in the past three years.

SECOND SEN. Truman has alienated every bloc of voters in the country.

FIRST SEN. No he hasn't. Harry will get more Negro votes than any candidate ever had.

THIRD SEN. Big deal! How many of them are there?

FIRST SEN. Enough to swing a national election.

SECOND SEN. Not when it costs the entire white South. So he lost that, then labor after the railroad fiasco, then his support in Congress. What has he done beside set a record for getting his picture taken?

THIRD SEN. Look at the farm situation.

FIRST SEN. Nobody could make that thing work. It isn't Harry's fault.

SECOND SEN. The farmer doesn't know that. He'll vote for a yellow dog before he votes Democratic this time.

THIRD SEN. Who's left to vote for Truman? Nobody.

FOURTH SEN. Do you think he'd take the nomination again?

THIRD SEN. Are you kidding? What else has he got, except to go back to the farm himself.

SECOND SEN. Then even Harry will vote Republican after he sees how bad his own ag program is. (*All laugh.*)

THIRD SEN. Sure he wants it. Only we can't afford him. Look what he's done to us in less than four years.

FIRST SEN. Boys, don't get me wrong. I don't say he's a world-beater.

SECOND SEN. Is he an anybody-beater? The public wants leadership. We've got to give them a new personality.

THIRD SEN. Who are you thinking about that is any better?

SECOND SEN. Hand me that phone book there. The first ten names I pick at random will get more votes.

FOURTH SEN. (*Rise, cross Downstage.*) Just for starters, Henry Wallace. He'll get that farm vote.

FIRST SEN. No, sir. Too liberal.

FOURTH SEN. Well, then, Jimmy Byrnes. He would give anything to run. Including his hat, eye-teeth, and umbrella.

SECOND SEN. He'd run for any office at any time. On either party.

THIRD SEN. Then let's hope the Republicans have a place for him.

SECOND SEN. What about Claude Pepper? There's the New Deal vote locked up.

THIRD SEN. That's no recommendation. You know what's left of that wing.

FOURTH SEN. McKellar has had a taste of power in the Senate.

THIRD SEN. He'd love the second slot, but I don't think Ken would take the top job.

SECOND SEN. That's good. I don't want him either. What about Happy Chandler, or maybe Paul Douglass? (*Pause.*)

FIRST SEN. I'm still listening for you to come up with the great white hope.

THIRD SEN. Then listen to this. What about George Marshall? Who can say anything against him?

FOURTH SEN. I can. Nobody except the Army knows him. A good man, yes; a real good man. (*Sits.*) He's just not electable.

THIRD SEN. What makes you so sure? He's never run for anything.

FOURTH SEN. That's why he's not electable.

Third Sen. I've got a possibility. (*Rises, crosses Downstage.*) This guy is better known than Mickey Mouse and personifies the old saw about dogs-church-flag-motherhood. Ike.

Second Sen. Ike Eisenhower?

Third Sen. You damn right. He's an American hero. How do you beat it?

Fourth Sen. I'll tell you how you beat it. He's also a general, and you know what the public thinks about that.

Second Sen. Are you guys even sure he's a Democrat?

Third Sen. Army officers haven't got any politics. That's a luxury they can't afford. (*Sits.*) All of a sudden he's a Democrat when we nominate him.

Second Sen. Maybe so. The Republicans won't even vote against him. He hasn't made anybody mad.

Fourth Sen. Some pretty prominent people are working on him: FDR, Jr., Dick Russell, and that young hot-shot mayor in Minneapolis. What's his name?

Second Sen. Herbert Humphrey?

Fourth Sen. Yeah. Now, who will we get to run with Ike? Don't anybody say "Truman."

Second Sen. What about Stevenson in Illinois? He's a comer.

Third Sen. Bill Fulbright might be good. Or the guy from South Carolina.

Fourth Sen. Strom Thurmond?

Third Sen. Yeah. He's got more ambition than a chorus girl.

Fourth Sen. Just about as much sense . . . And not as good a figure. If you back him, I quit.

Second Sen. Okay, okay. Who do you think the Republicans will pick?

Fourth Sen. Well, I hear there is new support for Stassen.

Third Sen. (*Incredibly.*) Oh, come on!

FOURTH SEN. Yeah. This time Mrs. Stassen is going to vote for him. (*All laugh.*) Okay. So maybe we go with Ike, huh, and worry about the second spot later?

FIRST SEN. (*Rises.*) I still go with Truman.

FOURTH SEN. (*Rises.*) If we do they'll beat us with their slogan: Had Enough?

SECOND SEN. While we are all singing— (*He rises and sings.*) I'm just *mild* about Harry.

(THIRD SEN. *rises, all cross Upstage to* HST's *desk. Four actors from Stage Right strike chairs to their original positions.* MATT *rises, crosses to desk.*)

MATT. Come in, gentlemen. (*He crosses to desk, sits.*)

HST. Hello, boys. I've seen a lot of customers today. They all talked down to me, so that I could understand. Sit down. (*Two* SENATORS *sit; others stand to Right and Left of* HST's *chair.*) What is it: old business or new?

THIRD SEN. A little of both, Mr. President.

HST. When you call me that, I can tell that this is serious. All right, *Senator,* I'll try to keep up. Shoot.

FOURTH SEN. Have you given any thought to running in '48?

HST. Hmmm. I'd call that both old and new business. I'm old, the business is new. Yes, I have.

SECOND SEN. Are you going to?

HST. Well, Bess is heartily opposed, so I haven't come to a firm decision. As Andy Jackson used to say, are you fur it or ag'in it?

FIRST SEN. My stand is absolutely unequivocal, Mr. President.

HST. Hold on. You've got to talk so a country boy can understand it.

FIRST SEN. Simply, I'm behind you 100%.

SECOND SEN. So am I, of course . . . ⎫
THIRD SEN. We all are, but . . . . ⎬ (*To-*
FOURTH SEN. I am too, however . . . ⎭ *gether.*)

HST. I hear a not-so-solid front. To quote a fellow out my way, when a man spends Sunday doing too much howling and praying, you had better lock your smoke house.

SECOND SEN. Harry, you've given more than is fair to ask of anyone in public office. Our concern is, if you're, uh, tired, if a large-scale campaign might be too much, then . . .

HST. I've made a few campaigns before.

THIRD SEN. Now is the time to get somebody ready, if you are, uh, undecided . . .

HST. What if I don't run? Who do you think can win?

FIRST SEN. *You* can, and I hope you'll run.

THIRD SEN. We all do, Harry. But if you don't, then we want to pump some new blood in the race. A Henry Wallace or . . .

HST. You say "new blood" and "Henry Wallace" in the same breath?

SECOND SEN. Well, Adlai Stevenson . . .

THIRD SEN. Ike, too.

HST. He's popular these days. Do we have any Democrats out in Kansas where he came from?

FOURTH SEN. Ask Alf Landon. (*All laugh.*)

THIRD SEN. Well, we think you can win, Harry. You know that. But if you are going to retire . . .

FOURTH SEN. Or if you're worried about your image, perhaps, or . . .

SECOND SEN. We don't want you to feel obligated if you . . .

HST. Let me say this. If I run, I'll run on my record and be proud of it. And I'll give it my damnedest for the party. (*He rises.*) So I thank you for coming over. Let me consider it and let you know. Don't sell me down the river before I've had a chance to throw my hat in the ring.

THIRD SEN. We wouldn't do that, Harry.

HST. If I decide to move from Pennsylvania Avenue, I'll do it without a national election making up

my mind for me. Good night. (*He crosses to Stage
Left, exits.* SENATORS *cross Downstage slowly, shaking heads, exchanging glances.*)

THIRD SEN. Well, hell!

(*BLACKOUT.* SENATORS *cross to chairs, sit.*)

SCENE 16

HST *enters, takes Right desk chair, crosses with it to
Downstage Right Center, takes off coat, places it
over back of chair, sits.* BESS *rises, takes Left
desk chair, crosses with it to Downstage Left
Center, sits. Actor or Stage hand brings small
table with table radio to Downstage Center between chairs.* BESS *has book.* BILL *rises, crosses to
lectern.*

BILL. Yes, sir, a lot of people wanted to give Harry
back to Missouri. But the old man had a job to finish.
He wanted to build a better America, he wasn't ready
to go home. And a lot *more* people wanted him to stay
in Washington, too. (*He crosses Upstage of Left of*
BESS. HST *leans toward radio, listens, fidgets.* BESS
looks at him, slightly annoyed.)

BESS. If you are *that* nervous, why don't you go
over to the convention hall?

BILL. Will there be anything else before I go, Mr.
President? (*Pause.*)

BESS. Harry.

HST. (*Finally diverting his attention from the
radio.*) What?

BESS. Bill asked you a question.

HST. What is it, Bill?

BILL. Do you need anything, sir?

HST. A few delegate votes is all. (*He returns his
attention to the radio.* BILL *starts to cross.*)

BESS. I do, Bill.

BILL. (*Turning to her.*) Yes, ma'am?

BESS. Get the convention to nominate someone else so that we can go home, will you?

BILL. I don't think they'd listen. Good night, Mrs. Truman, Mr. President.

BESS. Good night, Bill. (BILL *crosses to chair, sits.*)

HST. Alabama just walked out. I'll bet Sam Rayburn is a mad convention chairman over there right now.

BESS. Why did they?

HST. I don't know why. You've been so busy talking that I couldn't hear. (*He rises, takes several steps Downstage Right.*) Strom Thurmond has got a lot of support in the South. If the party nominates him, it is making a big mistake. (BESS *turns off radio.* HST *turns to her.*) Why did you do that? Turn it back on.

BESS. I will not have you sit here and get all riled up. (HST *crosses, sits, turns on radio.*) This could go on all night. Harry, will you go to bed and get some rest?

HST. Go to bed? Bess, I've got to know whether to go over and make an acceptance speech or not.

BESS. Well, I hope you won't have to. What thanks have you gotten for four years of hard work?

HST. Three and a half.

BESS. Nothing, except you look ten years older and are twenty years more tired. We can be at home with our friends, you can play the piano and go to the farm and be the elder statesman without worrying about foreign policy and the economy and . . .

HST. Sh! Phil Donnelly is nominating me. (*He rises.*) Listen to the applause! Listen, Bess! There are a lot of people who don't forget me. (BESS *turns off radio.* HST *is irritated.*)

BESS. Don't listen to all that and get an ulcer.

HST. (*Turns on radio.*) Do you think I can't take it? (*He paces, Downstage Right.*) When you've done what I've done, you make political enemies. I'll make a few more before I'm through. Like I always say, "if you can't stand the heat, get out of the kitchen."

BESS. (*Resigned.*) Like you always say.

HST. This cook stays right there next to the fire!

BESS. All right. Well, if you're sitting up, I am, too. (BESS *rises.*) I'll get my other who-done-it in the bedroom. (BESS *crosses to her Stage Left chair, picks up another book. HST listens intently to radio, smiles, turns radio off, sits back satisfied. BESS crosses to chair at Left Center, sits.*) Well, you turned the radio off. I'm glad.

HST. I turned it off, because it's all over. (*Pause, a beat. BESS looks at him.*)

BESS. I'm afraid to ask. Who won?

HST. Two hundred sixty-three votes for Dick Russell, (*He rises.*) 947½ votes for us. (BESS *rises, he hugs her.*) Bess, we won!

BESS. (*With mixed emotions, not altogether happy.*) I knew you would, cook. (*She turns away, takes several steps to Stage Left, as HST straightens tie, puts on coat.*)

HST. Well, I guess I'd better get over to the convention. (*Pause.*) What should I tell 'em?

BESS. Tell them that you accept. (*She looks at HST, smiles, crosses to him, takes his hand.*) No. Tell them that *we* do!

(*BLACKOUT. BESS and HST return chairs to their original positions flanking desk. Actor or stagehand strikes table and radio. BESS and HST cross to chairs, sit.*)

SCENE 17

BILL *sits, asleep, for about eight counts after lights are on him. He wakes suddenly, looks out at fourth wall startled, rises quickly, and hurriedly crosses to lectern.*

BILL. Oh. Excuse me. You'd have been tired too if you shagged after the old man day and night. Visiting, shaking hands, making maybe a dozen speeches every day: 30,000 miles to every whistlestop on every railroad. I mean I'm tired! Him? Huh! He's got more energy than a high-school kid.

It's getting so I can't sleep if the bed doesn't roll. But the next clown that calls me "porter" is going to catch it right in the mouth! (*Entire cast, except for* BILL, HST, MARGARET, *and* BESS *cross to Downstage to form crowd Scene, stand from Stage Right to Center Stage, facing* BILL, *listening.* BILL *speaks in oratorical style.*)

And so, citizens of Harlem, when you vote, remember Harry S. Truman's speech to Congress last February. The one where he asked for a bill outlawing Jim Crow in school and in transportation and in public facilities. He asked for a law against lynching. He means it when he says equality for all people and opportunity for everyone. I'm proud to present my friend, the President, and the next President of the United States. (HST *rises, crosses Downstage to lectern, shakes hands with* BILL *as crowd cheers.* BILL *crosses to chair, sits.*)

HST. Thank you, Bill. Thank you, fellow Americans. We've done a lot of travelling lately to let the people know what is going on, and to hear what they want from their government. We've learned that they like our programs. They like the Democratic party because it is for the little man. They know that they can't let those mothbag, I mean moss-back, Republicans run things. (*He and crowd laugh.*) I guess either of those terms is correct.

MAN. Lay it on, Harry. Give 'em hell!

HST. I will! I intend to! We've got to do better than

that do-nothing no-account Republican Congress. Some of us stay-at-home Democrats brought that bunch on ourselves by not getting out and voting.

Now is not the time to quit. It is time to get your government to do what's right. (*Cheers by crowd.*) And now, I want you to meet The Boss. (BESS *rises, crosses Downstage to* HST's *right. He puts his arm around her, she smiles at crowd who cheer.*) She doesn't like that name, even if it's what she is. (BESS *frowns good-naturedly at* HST.) Mrs. T. doesn't speak in public, but she sure does a lot of it in private. (*Laughs and cheers from crowd.*) And here's the one who bosses her. (*He looks around.*) Where's Margaret? (MARGARET *rises, crosses Downstage to* HST's *left as crowd cheers. She smiles at* HST *and crowd.*) Hi, honey.

Well, we've made 351 speeches. Not really speeches, but visits with people. Now we're going home and vote, and know you are going to do what's right.

I'm not asking you to vote for me. I want you to get out and vote for yourselves—for your own interest, your own part of the country, and your own friends.

(*Crowd cheers, turn their backs on the fourth wall and face Upstage, standing in place. BLACKOUT. HST, BESS, and* MARGARET *cross to Upstage Center.*)

SCENE 18

BILL *rises, crosses to lectern.*

BILL. He had the common touch, huh? When he speaks, you *know* he is talking to *you*. That man is so good you'd think he was black.

How do you beat it? You don't. Ask the Republicans. They know all about the biggest political upset in history. (BILL *picks up newspaper, looks at it, shakes his head. HST, BESS, MARGARET cross to Downstage Center as crowd turns, faces HST. BILL crosses to HST, hands him newspaper.*) Congratulations, Mr. President. Read this instead of the Kansas City "Star."

(HST *unfolds paper, looks at it, laughs, holds up Chicago "Tribune" to fourth wall to show headlines:* "Dewey Defeats Truman." *Crowd laughs.*)

HST. Why, I thought I won! (*Crowd laughs.*) The old Literary Digest of '36, made a little prediction about Landon, too.

MATT. (*He crosses Downstage to HST.*) Here is a telegram for you, Mr. President.

HST. (*He takes wire, opens and reads it.*) "My congratulations on your election as President of the United States. I urge all Americans to unite behind you toward building a greater America. Signed, Thomas E. Dewey." (*Not reading.*) That's right nice of Mr. Dewey. I know he means it.

This is not a time for Republicans and Democrats. We need everybody in the common cause. I want your help and cooperation. Then this great country which God has chosen to lead the world to peace and prosperity will succeed in that undertaking.

(*Crowd cheers. BLACKOUT. All cross to chairs, sit.*)

SCENE 19

BILL *rises, crosses to lectern.*

BILL. President Truman was glad to keep that title for another four years. Things went pretty smooth for him until June of 1950. He had fun being Mr. Citizen, too, 'though he didn't get much opportunity. Even when he went home, the office followed the man. (HST *crosses to Downstage Left Center. He is coatless.* BILL *removes coat, takes two garden rakes from Left wings, hands one to* HST *as both rake and sometimes lean on them.* VAUGHAN, *without coat, but sleeves rolled and tie loosened, rises, crosses to* HST, *looks at him curiously.*) Morning, General Vaughan.

VAUGHAN. Harry, what in the devil are you doing?

HST. If you had ever done it, you'd know.

VAUGHAN. What time did you say for tonight?

HST. Oh, about eight. We'll teach them how we play poker in Missouri.

VAUGHAN. You found some pigeons, huh? Good. Say, let me ask you something.

HST. It goes one pair, two pair, three of a kind . . .

VAUGHAN. Just for that, I'll take your money, too.

HST. You try it!

VAUGHAN. Unfortunately, I have. (*Crosses to* HST, *puts hand on his shoulder.*) Harry, are you going to run in '52?

HST. (*Stops raking, looks at* VAUGHAN *incredibly.*) Have you lost your mind?

VAUGHAN. (*Subdued.*) Well, I just thought I'd ask. (*He shrugs, crosses to chair, sits.*)

BILL. Mr. President, you'd better take a little rest.

HST. Rest? This *is* rest. I don't get to do this at the White House.

BILL. Yes, sir. But Mrs. Truman says for you to get off the front lawn looking like that.

HST. Well, you tell her to get out of the kitchen looking like she does.

BILL. If you don't mind, you tell her.

HST. (*Stops raking, leans on it.*) Maybe we'd better forget it. Boy, it's good to be home again. (*He looks around.*) Have I lost my shadow?

BILL. No, sir. Nick is on the front porch, like a watch dog.

HST. That's the farthest he's been away from me in five years.

ROSE. (ROSE CONWAY *rises, speaks in place.*) Mr. President, Margaret is on the phone from New York.

HST. Tell her I have a very important agriculture matter pending, Rose. I'll call her back.

ROSE. Yes, sir. (*She sits.* TOURIST *rises, crosses to Downstage Right, calls to* HST.)

TOURIST. Hey, buddy, this where Truman lives?

HST. That's right.

TOURIST. I guess he's in Washington. How 'bout you standing over there so's I can get a pitcher.

HST. Okay. Where?

TOURIST. Just don't block the front porch. (HST *moves several paces to Stage Left.*) Bring your helper with you.

BILL. (*He crosses to* HST, *speaks quietly to him.*) Should I tell him?

HST. Not on your life.

TOURIST. We're from Montana, visitin' folks in Omaha. Drove 255 mile out of my way down here to see it. I voted for Harry, guess I can take a pitcher of his house. Hold it right there. Smile a little. (HST *puts his arm around* BILL, *as* TOURIST *pantomimes taking a picture.*) That's good. Thanks a lot, buddy. (TOURIST *waves, crosses to chair, sits.*)

BILL. I'd give a pretty to be there when he shows that picture, and have his neighbor say "that ain't a gardner—that's the President".

HST. I'll bet you fifty cents that the neighbor is a Republican. (*He rakes contentedly.*)

MATT. (*He rises, crosses to* HST, *carries message, speaks excitedly.*) Mr. President! Mr. President!

HST. Out here, Matt.

MATT. We just got this message broken.

HST. While I read it, you exercise this rake a little. (*He hands* MATT *the rake, takes message from him.*) You didn't think this was a vacation, did you?

MATT. You won't either.

HST. (*He reads message, becomes serious.*) You're

right, Matt. Tell the boys to get the Sacred Cow ready. We'll be at the airport in an hour.

MATT. Yes, sir. (*He crosses to chair, sits.* BESS *rises, speaks in place.*)

BESS. Harry? Harry. What do you want Vieta to fix for dinner?

HST. (*Jaw set, faces fourth wall, determined.*) I want those North Korean communist sons of bitches roasted over an open fire.

(*BLACKOUT.* HST *gets coat, crosses to Stage Left, exits.*)

SCENE 20

BILL *puts on coat, crosses to lectern. Stage Right actors rise, bring chairs toward Center Stage into sight lines as necessary. The three Downstage actors, and actor playing* ADMIRAL KING *in Scene 9, strike chairs to Right wings, exit. Stage Right actors confer silently while standing during* BILL'S *lines, each sits as his name is called. Desk Right chair is placed at head of "table" as in Scene 9.*

BILL. He interrupted his Armed Forces Council from their Sunday activities, too. Summoned from gardening and golf were Secretary of State Acheson, U. N. Ambassador Jessup, Secretary of Defense Johnson, Secretary of the Navy Matthews: Secretary of Air Finletter, and the Joint Chiefs of Staff: Generals Bradley, Collins and Vandenberg, and Admiral Sherman. (BILL *crosses to chair, sits.*)

ACHESON. How did we get a unanimous vote out of the Security Council?

JESSUP. The only possible way: the Russians were absent. The U. N. labeled the Korean aggression a breach of peace. Telling them to withdraw will show the world we mean business.

JOHNSON. Now we've got to back it up.

SHERMAN. Who is "we" beside the United States?

JESSUP. Other members of the U. N.

JOHNSON. Anyone other than us is going to be problemmatical.

JESSUP. There's the Republic of Korea military.

JOHNSON. Change my last statement to "damned
problemmatical"!

BRADLEY. Our own strength is far from what it
should be. The Navy is down to . . .

MATTHEWS. Against my continued pro-
tests that we do not . . .   *(To-*
SHERMAN. In spite of my repeatedly   *gether.)*
pointing out that . . .

BRADLEY. We're aware of that!

VANDENBERG. Our Air Force is down some, but not
to a serious point.

SHERMAN. (*To* JOHNSON.) Lou, when in the hell will
you listen to someone other than the Air Force?

JOHNSON. The President wanted an economy peacetime budget, the first one in ten years.

SHERMAN. Now that we need an immediate striking
force, he's paid a damn big price to get it. Can't you
tell him anything?

BRADLEY. Don't think the Navy is alone. The Army
has less than 600,000 men, all with out-dated World
War II weapons.

COLLINS. That's less than half our strength at Pearl
Harbor.

JOHNSON. We'll commit what we can of what we've
got, if the President says to.

SHERMAN. I knew that this 38th parallel business
with the Soviets wouldn't work. (*He rises.*) Whoever
the hell made that decision was . . .

BRADLEY. (*Rises, speaks sharply.*) Admiral, the
Commander in Chief did. (*Both sit.*)

ACHESON. Gentlemen, if we are going to prevent a
third world war, we have to draw a line somewhere.

HST. (*He enters, Stage Left, crosses to desk Right
chair. All rise.*) We draw it here. Keep your seats.

(*All sit after* HST *does.*) I followed your suggestions and advised MacArthur to evacuate all U. S. personnel.

BRADLEY. Civilian and military, Mr. President?

HST. Our military advisors are remaining. Mac is to make ammunition and supplies available to the ROK. Admiral, what is the size of our Seventh Fleet there?

SHERMAN. Task Force 77 has less than 200 ships.

MATTHEWS Mr. President, can we commission more ships for Far East duty?

HST. I want to see what develops first. MacArthur says that the South Koreans are getting the hell beat out of them, so it may be necessary. If it doesn't act with a strong repelling force, the U. N. is dead.

SHERMAN. Now will you let us re-build the Navy? We haven't got enough punch left to . . .

HST. (*Tersely.*) Admiral, if we'd known this would happen, we'd have done a lot of things differently. What MacArthur needs from us, he'll get. Is that clear?

SHERMAN. (*Mumbles.*) Yes, sir.

HST. Thank you, gentlemen. I know you'd rather have spent your Sunday some other way. So would I. Everything I've done in the past five years has been to avoid making the decision I had to make tonight.

(*All rise. BLACKOUT. Actors return chairs to original position.* HST *places his chair to Right of desk. Actors who exited to Right wings during this Scene enter with chairs, all sit.*)

SCENE 21

BILL *rises, crosses to lectern, reads from newspaper.*

BILL. "October, 1950. General MacArthur says we have regained the initiative in Korea." (*He crosses to*

chair, sits. Three REPORTERS *rise, cross to Downstage
Right Center.* MATT *rises, crosses to Center Stage.)*

MATT. Ladies and gentlemen, the President of the
United States. (HST *rises, crosses to Downstage
Center.)*

FIRST REPORTER. Mr. President, recently there have
been good reports from Korea.

HST. Yes. Sixteen nations are now with us.

SECOND REPORTER. What has been the experience
with the called-up National Guard and reservists?

HST. They are integrated into regular units and
doing a good job. Don't put down our so-called weekend warriors.

THIRD REPORTER. Mr. President, you have been
criticized in some papers . . .

HST. But not yours, surely!

THIRD REPORTER. Of course not, sir. (*All laugh.*)
The criticism has been for activating these civilian
soldiers.

HST. I'm not concerned about what people think of
me as long as we're on the right track. And we are.
Next question.

SECOND REPORTER. Mr. President, certain polls show
that your popularity is at an all-time low. Do you care
to comment on that?

HST. (*He crosses several steps Downstage.*) I have
never known fighting to be popular. I'll worry about
the polls some other time. (*He turns, faces* REPORTERS.)
I'm not going to turn a deaf ear to our top military
professionals and listen to some disgruntled Republicans. (REPORTERS *laugh,* HST *takes several steps
Upstage.*)

FIRST REPORTER. What is the extent of our com-
mitment in Korea?

HST. To stop the communists from further aggression.

SECOND REPORTER. Mr. President, why not hit their
industry north of the 38th parallel?

HST. The industrial facilities are Russia and Red China. Does that answer your question? (REPORTERS *laugh*.)

THIRD REPORTER. So this is a limited action?

HST. Yes.

SECOND REPORTER. Then the objectives are also limited?

HST. That's right. All we want is to protect the Republic of Korea from aggression.

FIRST REPORTER. Does General MacArthur agree?

HST. The general understands the Far East better than anyone. But this limited warfare concept is new to him, too. When he recovered Seoul, I sent him a message of our thanks for a job well and nobly done. That shows you my regard for General MacArthur.

THIRD REPORTER. Mr. President, everybody keeps asking: are we, or are we not at war?

HST. We are *not* at war.

SECOND REPORTER. Could you elaborate on that statement, sir?

HST. Yes. The Republic of Korea was unlawfully attacked by a bunch of bandits from North Korea. The United Nations is suppressing that bandit raid. That is all there is to it.

FIRST REPORTER. Would it be correct to call it a police action?

HST. That is exactly what it amounts to. (*Pause, as* REPORTERS *write*.)

MATT. Any further questions?

REPORTERS. Thank you, Mr. President.

(*BLACKOUT. All cross to chairs, sit.*)

SCENE 22

BILL *rises, crosses to lectern*.

BILL. Korea went on for two more years. The White House was a busy place. I wished I was on vacation.

I mean a *real* one, not like Independence. The old man was getting mad, and that's when I wanted to be out of his way. But Senator Jenner came to do battle. (*He crosses, sits.* JENNER *rises, speaks in place angrily as he yells Upstage to* MATT, *who rises.*)

JENNER. Connelly! Where is he? I told him I was coming over!

MATT. Go right on in, Senator. (*He sits,* JENNER *crosses to Right of desk.* HST *looks up from writing.*)

HST. Morning, Bill. Sit down.

JENNER. I won't be that long. What's this about MacArthur?

HST. I can't tolerate his insubordination any longer.

JENNER. Who the hell are you to argue with a general who knows that Oriental picture backwards and forwards? (*He crosses several steps Downstage.*)

HST. I'm Commander-in-Chief of the Armed Forces, that's who the hell.

JENNER. (*Turns, points at* HST, *crosses Upstage to Right of desk.*) And you know more about it than he does?

HST. About our policies, yes. He carries them out, only he hasn't.

JENNER. He's the greatest military leader of our time, maybe all time.

HST. I don't doubt his ability. I also don't doubt his cooperation. He doesn't have any.

JENNER. (*Crosses several steps Downstage.*) You've already got enough public opposition to your banana war. (*Turns, crosses Upstage to Right of desk.*) Harry, there are going to be a lot of Republicans in Congress damn mad if you take action on him.

HST. I don't plan to send a bill to the Senate on it.

JENNER. We've been bipartisan on your foreign policy, don't forget.

HST. (*Rises, places hands on desk, leans toward* JENNER.) Foreign policy is no place for politics.

JENNER. (*Hands on desk, leans toward* HST.) It is, if the policy isn't any good. It won't be worth a damn if you can MacArthur. He's doing his best on your silly idea of containment of the Reds, or whatever the hell it is.

HST. All right! (*Mad, straightens, crosses around Left of desk to Downstage of it.*) You go tell that handful of hard-headed Republicans that I sent this to MacArthur not an hour ago. (HST *takes paper from desk, reads.*) "I deeply regret that it becomes my duty as President and Commander-in-Chief of the United States military forces to replace you— (JENNER *puts hands on hips.*) as Supreme Commander, Allied Powers; and Commanding General, U. S. Army, Far East. You will turn over your commands, effective at once, to Lieutenant General Matthew B. Ridgway." (*Not reading.*) Now Bill, have you got any questions?

JENNER. (*Crosses toward chair, points at HST, speaks over his shoulder.*) You'll have a lot of them tomorrow.

(JENNER *sits. BLACKOUT.* HST *crosses to chair, sits.*)

SCENE 23

BILL *rises, crosses to lectern, reads from newspaper.*

BILL. "Arriving home for the first time in fourteen years, General Douglas MacArthur said: 'The only politics I have is contained in the simple phrase known well by all of you: God Bless America.'

"The general is on his way to address a joint session of Congress at the invitation of the Speaker of the House, Joe Martin." (*Not reading.*) He's here in Washington now, and so is everybody else. You can't get anywhere in this traffic. (*He reads.*) "It is not known if Senator Jenner will follow his ringing pronouncement on the floor this morning that our only choice is to impeach President Truman." (*He puts down newspaper.*)

I wish the old man hadn't had to recall Mac. Everybody in the country has written him about it, and I've had to carry every sack of that mail. Well, MacArthur made his speech. I'll have to admit it was a good one. Remember it? (*He speaks oratorically.*) "I thank you for this last great honor in the fading twilight of my life.

I still remember the refrain which proclaimed most proudly that old soldiers never die, they just fade away. And like the old soldier, I now close my military career and just fade away, an old soldier who tried to do his duty as God gave him the light to see that duty. Goodbye." (*He speaks conversationally.*) Yes, sir, some speech. Like he said, MacArthur faded away. General Ridgway did a good job over there. He fought a successful limited war, just like the Commander-in-Chief wanted. (DEMOCRATS NOS. 1 *and* 2 *rise, cross to Downstage Right.*) But, as always, some people weren't satisfied. Maybe because it was another election year: 1952.

(*BLACKOUT.* BILL *crosses to chair, sits.*)

SCENE 24

DEMOCRATS NOS. 1 *and* 2 *cross from Downstage Right to Downstage Left. During the Scene all cross slowly to Stage Left.*

FIRST DEMOCRAT. How's your campaign coming?

SECOND DEMOCRAT. All right, if I weren't a Democrat. How's yours?

FIRST DEMOCRAT. When I was home last week, I reminded them to keep my name on the law firm stationery. That's how it's coming.

SECOND DEMOCRAT. I know what you mean. It's pretty hard to disassociate yourself from things like Harry Vaughan, no action from that egg-head Stevenson, and Truman's smart-mouth comments.

THIRD DEMOCRAT. (*He rises, crosses to others, who turn, listen.*) I don't notice you thumbing your nose at some other things like the Truman Doctrine and NATO and the Marshall Plan.

FIRST DEMOCRAT. Then was then. What has he done to brag about lately? Did you ever try to wind up a speech with— (*Speaks in oratorical style.*) "and isn't it wonderful how things are going in Korea?"

THIRD DEMOCRAT. This has been a good four years. I'll hitch my wagon to Harry's term any day.

FIRST DEMOCRAT. That's easy enough for you to say. You don't come up for re-election 'til '54.

SECOND DEMOCRAT. Well, if either of you walk by here and see a tired old man selling apples, buy one. I'll need the business.

(DEMOCRATS *exit, Stage Left, cross around backdrop to chairs, sit. BLACKOUT.*)

SCENE 25

An angry HST sits behind desk. An uncomfortable Major General VAUGHAN *sits in desk Right chair.*

HST. And another thing, *General* Vaughan. What about that steel deal?

VAUGHAN. What steel deal?

HST. You know good and well. There is a top priority on construction steel. And you okayed a request for somebody out in California.

VAUGHAN. Oh, that.

HST. Yes, that! Do you know what he used it for?

VAUGHAN. He told me he was going to build a . . .

HST. Do you know where that steel went?

VAUGHAN. (*Soft.*) Into a grandstand at a race track. But, Harry . . .

HST. People can't get the stuff for housing and you authorized a damn race track!

VAUGHAN. (*Defensively louder.*) I don't have that power. I just introduced him by letter is all.

HST. On White House stationery! What did you get from the race track guy for that favor?

VAUGHAN. (*Loud, incensed, rises.*) That's a hell of an accusation! You know me better than that.

HST. Then explain the deep freeze.

VAUGHAN. (*Soft.*) Uh, it was a present. I didn't know it was coming. I went home, and two guys were putting it in my kitchen. (*Loud.*) What would you have done? Send it back?

HST. (*Rises.*) I've told you this a hundred times, and I'm going to tell you again. Quit using this address as a meeting place for all your half-assed buddies. Now is that clear, or do you want me to spell it out?

VAUGHAN. Harry, you know I wouldn't do anything to put you in a bad light.

HST. (*Softens, as both sit.*) Harry, damn it, I know it, but it looks bad. Every paper in the country has a cartoon of you cooling your butt in that deep freeze.

VAUGHAN. The press made a big thing out of nothing.

HST. It looks like hell. We've had no scandal in eight years. I mean to keep it that way.

VAUGHAN. If we could only do something about McCarthy.

HST. That bastard! According to him, everybody in the government is a communist. He tells more lies and slanders more good character than anyone I ever saw. (*Pause.*) Okay. Are we square?

VAUGHAN. I've got the picture. (*He rises.*) You want me to send in Stevenson?

HST. Yes. As if I didn't have enough to do besides getting him elected.

VAUGHAN. Come in, Governor. (*Democratic Presidential candidate* ADLAI STEVENSON *rises, crosses to* VAUGHAN, *shake hands.*) How is the next President of the United States?

STEVENSON. Not too well. We need all the help we can get.

VAUGHAN. If there is anything you want from the White House . . . (*He looks around sheepishly at* HST, *who looks admonishingly at him.*) I mean, if I can help, let me know. (*He crosses to chair, sits.* STEVENSON *crosses to Right of desk, offers his hand which* HST *declines.*)

STEVENSON. Hello, Mr. Pres . . .

HST. You know less about running a campaign than anybody I ever saw.

STEVENSON. Oh?

HST. What's the best asset in any race?

STEVENSON. There are a lot of them.

HST. There's only one. Time. And you have frittered it away like you have forever.

STEVENSON. (*Sits.*) Well, now, I've made a lot of speeches and public . . .

HST. Look. I hand-picked you in January, invited you here to . . .

STEVENSON. Harry, it's common knowledge that you wanted Fred Vinson.

HST. You didn't let me finish. I started to say, after Fred decided to stay on the Court. You went home to think about it. How the hell long does that take? (*Rises, crosses to Left of desk.*) Maybe a week, maybe two. In March—March!—you said no. You said no to the top job in the country.

STEVENSON. I was waiting to see what would happen to Barkley and Harriman and Russell.

HST. You saw. So then you came out with that bunk about an unlikely draft. And they did, in the first real draft we've had in the Democratic party in seventy-two years. (HST *crosses to Downstage Left Center.* STEVENSON *rises, follows.*)

STEVENSON. I've been in this race all the way ever since. I've hardly seen my law office.

HST. When are you opening your headquarters in Washington?

STEVENSON. (*Reluctantly.*) I'm not.

HST. New York, then?

STEVENSON. I'm going to keep it in Springfield.

HST. Springfield? (*He crosses Upstage to desk.*) Who the hell ever heard of a Presidential campaign headquarters in Springfield!

STEVENSON. Everybody will soon.

HST. Nobody will. Ever. That isn't the center of anything! (*He crosses Downstage Center, paces.*) So you're going to sit out there and . . .

STEVENSON. (*Firmly.*) I'm not going to sit anyplace. I plan to hit every single state.

HST. Well, wherever you're going you'll make those lofty damn comments people can't understand.

STEVENSON. I speak to the people.

HST. You better do some listening, and find out what they want to know. I did it in '48, and we put a lot of arm-chair politicians out of business that year.

STEVENSON. You didn't have a Korea then, either.

HST. So now you do. (*He crosses Upstage, sits on desk.*) You think Eisenhower doesn't? I'll fix his wagon but good on my whistlestop next month.

STEVENSON. (*Brightens, crosses, puts his hand on* HST's *shoulder.*) I didn't know you were planning one, Harry. That's . . .

HST. Clear to the coast. When I said at the convention that we have nominated a winner, I didn't think I'd have to make you one all by myself.

STEVENSON. I'm very grateful. Now about Eisenhower . . .

HST. I'm going to tell the voters that Eisenhower

betrayed the foreign policy he helped establish. And that damn speech he made about— (*He speaks in mocking voice.*) I will go to Korea. (*Normally.*) Anyone who talks like a superman is a fraud. Now, maybe you don't want me to make this speech trip?

STEVENSON. (*Crosses to desk Right chair, sits. HST crosses, sits on desk.*) Of course I do. It would be an immense help.

HST. Everything you've done has been to divorce yourself from my administration.

STEVENSON. Harry, I want to project my own image, not to be a carbon copy of you. I want to clean up this mess in Washington.

HST. (*Pointed, rising.*) We've got no mess in Washington, Stevenson. This administration is clean. Don't toss off the past sixteen years of right good leadership to this country.

STEVENSON. I didn't mean that like it sounded, Harry.

HST. Another thing. (*He points at shoe with hole in it which is visible to house.*) Before you go back to your national headquarters in Springfield, get yourself a new pair of shoes.

(STEVENSON *looks at hole in shoe. BLACKOUT. STEVENSON and HST rise, cross to chairs, sit.*)

SCENE 26

BILL *rises, crosses to lectern.*

BILL. Stevenson couldn't make it in his old shoes. General Eisenhower was a mighty attractive candidate. But either way it would have turned out, it was moving day for us.

A lot of us are going home, including a President, or rather an ex-President. All those doubters who screamed about a shallow Truman and his light-weight buddies have another think coming. (BILL *picks up a book*.) Like this fellow writes about him. (*He reads*.) "He was an ordinary man, not an average man. He put an indelible imprint of greatness on the Presidency." (BILL *closes book*.) This small-town man, who went broke as a necktie seller, changed the course of the country for the better, and with it, world history. What a man! What a man! (*He crosses to chair, sits*. REPORTERS *rise, cross to Downstage Center*. HST *rises, crosses to Downstage Left Center*.)

SECOND REPORTER. Mr. President, what do you look forward to in private life?

HST. Taking my morning walks without being shadowed by a secret service man. But I did appreciate those fellows being there that morning in front of Blair House. If it weren't for them, those Puerto Ricans might have got me.

FIRST REPORTER. Was that the most frightening moment of your Presidency?

HST. No. The scaredest I was was one time in L. A. at the corner of Hollywood and Vine. I knew that eighty percent of the kooks in the country were within a two-mile radius. (REPORTERS *laugh*.)

THIRD REPORTER. Do you have any plans for retirement?

HST. No plans. The tragedy of too many men in office is that they don't know when to quit. (*He pauses, smiles*.) I might run for the Senate again when I'm ninety-one.

FIRST REPORTER. Would you like to be best remembered for the Truman Doctrine, the Berlin Blockade, your immediate recognition of Israel, or . . .

HST. I hope to be remembered as the people's President.

FOURTH REPORTER. Sir, there is talk of erecting a monument to you here in Washington.

HST. No thanks. A person may do something before

he dies that will make the people want to tear it down. (REPORTERS *laugh.*)

FIRST REPORTER. Do you, Mr. President, have any regrets about your major decisions?

HST. As Mrs. Truman and I leave the White House, we have none.

FIRST REPORTER. Any other comments?

HST. I guess not, except to thank you fellows for your courtesies during these past eight years.

A President is at liberty to be as great a man as he can. (*He strolls several steps.*) That reminds me of an epitaph I saw on a tombstone in Arizona. It said: "Here lies Jack Williams. He done his damnedest." I hope somebody can say that about me.

REPORTERS. Thank you, Mr. President. (REPORTERS *cross to Upstage Right.* MARGARET *and* BESS *rise, cross Downstage to* HST *on each side of him.* MARGARET *kisses him on the cheek.*)

MARGARET. Hi, *Mister* Truman!

HST. (*He laughs, puts his arm around her.*) Margie, in 1922, before you were born and before I was a country judge, was the last time anybody called me "mister."

RAYBURN. (*He rises, crosses Downstage to Right of* HST.) You don't think I'm going to call you that, do you?

HST. You never heard me say "Mister Rayburn" either, you told Texas coyote.

RAYBURN. Harry, history will be kind to you. They are going to forget the few times you didn't take dead aim, and shot from the hip. They are going to remember the great things you have done.

HST. It wasn't because I was a great President, but I had a good time trying to be one.

RAYBURN. Best of luck.

HST. Thanks, Sam. (*They shake hands.* RAYBURN *crosses to Upstage Right by* REPORTERS. *Senator* ROBERT A. TAFT *rises, crosses to* HST *who is happily surprised to see him.*) Well, well, well! When Senator Taft comes to the White House, this *is* a special day!

TAFT. It breaks precedent that I don't have an ax to grind, Harry.

HST. Bob, you old . . . (*He looks at* MARGARET *and* BESS, *speaks quietly.*) bastard. (MARGARET *and* BESS *look at* HST *admonishingly.*) You were the best antagonist any President ever had. At least you kept me honest.

TAFT. Hmmm. I'm not sure I've done a very good job.

HST. (*Kidding, in mock anger.*) Get out of here! Come see me in Missouri, will you?

TAFT. Best of everything, Harry.

HST. Thanks, Bob. (*They shake hands.*) You know, for a Republican, you're all right. (TAFT *waves, crosses to Upstage Right with* REPORTERS. BILL *rises, crosses to Left of* HST *with message.*)

BILL. Mr. President, you've got a message from Mr. Churchill.

HST. Give it to General Eisenhower. (*To* BESS.) Are you ready, Bess?

BILL. It's a personal message to you.

HST. All right. Read it.

BILL. (*Reading.*) "The last time we sat across a table together, I held you in very low esteem. Now I must tell you that you and you alone saved western civilization from communism. When the communists were knocking at the doors of Greece, you made the decision that saved that country from despair and destruction. When the communists threatened to take over devastated Europe, you provided the aid of America to save it with the Marshall Plan. When the communists blockaded Berlin, you ordered the airlift to keep it alive. When the communists threatened the Middle East, you provided help. And when the communists threatened the freedom of Korea and with it the freedom of the Far East, you and you alone, Mr.

President, made the decision to provide the strength to defeat it. I honor you, sir." (*Pause.* BESS *puts her hand on* HST's *arm as she and* MARGARET *look at him proudly.*)

HST. That's quite a tribute. I'll write Winston my thanks from Independence. (*Pause.* HST *looks around, shrugs.*) Well, Bess, this morning I woke up as President of the United States. Now I'll go to bed as a private citizen. I think I'll like it.

BESS. So will I. (*Entire company crosses to Downstage Right.*)

BILL. Could I say something, Mr. President?

HST. Shoot, Bill. What's on your mind?

BILL. A lot more than this, but my people know that *you* let our dime buy a ride in the *front* of the bus. (*Pause.* BILL *and* HST *look at each other in understanding and friendship, shake hands.*)

HST. Thanks, Bill.

BESS. (*Looking at crowd, Stage Right.*) Harry! Look at that! That crowd out there. They've come to say goodbye to you. (*There are cheers from the crowd.*) You've got to say something to them.

HST. (*He holds up both arms to acknowledge cheers.*) I appreciate this more than any meeting I ever attended as President or Vice President or Senator. This is the first time you have ever sent me home in a blaze of glory. I can't adequately express my appreciation. But I'll never forget it if I live to be a hundred. (*Pause. He smiles.*) And that's just what I expect to do! (*Crowd cheers.* HST *holds up his arms.* BESS *takes his hand, smiles at him.*)

BESS. Come on, Harry. Let's go home.

(HST, BESS, MARGARET, *and* BILL *cross to Stage Right, shaking hands with crowd, exchanging good wishes, waving.*)

CURTAIN—END OF ACT TWO

PRODUCTION NOTES

This documentary drama is best staged in the presentational style of chamber theatre. It is played in French Scenes. The only curtains are at the end of the Two Acts. With few exceptions, all cast members remain on Stage throughout the performance. There are only rare entrances and exits. Cast members rise, cross to the required Stage area, then return and sit in chairs at the end of Scenes, usually during Black-outs. Hand props are either held by actors or placed under chairs (as well as on or under Bill's lectern) where they are accessible.

Chair assignments are permanent. They can be out of the sight lines if playing room on Stage is limited. Chairs at Stage Right (from Upstage to Downstage) are for Stimson, Marshall, Leahy, King, Arnold, Conant, Compton, Scientist (assigned for the playing of Scene 9), plus four other actors who exit and strike their chairs during Scenes 9 and 20. Chairs at Stage Left (from Upstage to Downstage) are for Bess, Margaret, Mama Truman, Girl, and Rose. Separated slightly Downstage from them is Bill's chair.

At Upstage Left is a desk and chair, occupied by Matt, who faces Left wings. At slightly Left of Upstage Center is the desk and chair of HST, with arm chairs adjacent to Stage Left and Right of the desk. Upstage from the desk are the American and Presidential flags. The Presidential flag is not authorized; substitute the National Guard flag which will look authentic hanging on its staff.

Total Stage properties: nineteen straight-back chairs, two arm chairs, an arm chair on rollers for HST, HST's desk, Matt's desk, the two flags, lectern at Downstage Left for Bill, small table and radio to be set for Scene 16.

Hand/desk props include a box of strawberries, official-looking documentary papers for HST's and Matt's desks, citation for Scene 7, Kansas City "Stars" for Bill and HST's desks, two books for Bess, book on the lectern for Bill, Chicago "Tribune" with headline reading "DEWEY DEFEATS TRUMAN," cane, pads and pencils for Scene 9, Washington "Post," two rakes, two baseballs, medal on around-the-neck ribbon, desk pens, telephone, and equipment for HST's and

Matt's desks, telegram for Matt, four napkins, Bible, Reporters' scratch pads, several typed speeches for HST, Biddle's note to HST, and small autograph book for Girl. There are no cameras; the taking of pictures is pantomime.

Only twenty actors are required. Except for Girl, all are mature. Bill is a Negro. A few, more or less, may be used at the discretion of the director, depending on his multiple use of players and the size of the Stage. Male cast members should wear dark suits, white shirts and long ties, with exceptions listed below. No costume changes are made, although the removal of coats and rolling up of sleeves is done as stated in the script.

Costumes exceptions to the above are as follows:

HST—white double-breasted suit and conservative bow tie, glasses

Bess—knee-length comfortable suit, white blouse

Mrs. Roosevelt/Rose—knee-length comfortable suit

Girl—blouse, knee-length skirt, sloppy-joe sweater, bobby-sox, saddle shoes

Margaret—knee-length light-hue dress, not flashy

Mama Truman—mature-looking dress and shoes for elderly lady

Female cast members wear conservative dark suits or dresses.

The following cast members play single-character roles: HST, Bess, Mama Truman, Girl, Bill, Matt, and Margaret.

It is recommended that these cast members play multiple roles, with characters and Scenes listed (Scene numbers in parentheses) as follows:

Early (1), Stimson (4, 9), Second Reporter (7), Whitney (11), Johnson (20), Stevenson (25)

Kilgore (1), Second Republican (6), Marshall (8, 9), Griffith (14), Sherman (20)

Stone (1), Ed (5), Leahy (9), Vandenberg (20)

Rayburn (1, 2, 26), Second Reporter (5), Byrnes (7), King (9)

Fulbright (3), Third Reporter (5), Arnold (9), First Democrat (24), Acheson (20)

Anderson (3), First Republican (6), Conant (9), Second Democrat (15), Collins (20)

Vaughan (3, 19, 25), Third Republican (6), Compton (9), Johnston (11), Bradley (20)

Second Reporter (1), First Reporter (5), Cranston (7),
    Scientist (9), Jessup (20), Jenner (22), Second Reporter
    (26)
First Lady (3), Second Reporter (21), Third Reporter (26)
Second Lady (3), Fourth Republican (6), Third Democrat
    (15), First Reporter (21), Third Democrat (24), Fourth
    Reporter (26)
First Reporter (1), First Reporter (7), Biffle (12), Fourth
    Democrat (15), Matthews (20), Third Reporter (21),
    Second Democrat (24), First Reporter (26)
McKellar (2), Third Reporter (7), Charlie (5), Man (17),
    Tourist (19), Taft (26)
Mrs. Roosevelt (1), Rose (8, 19)

Entire company is in Scenes 17, 18, and 26. Most have
no lines.

Except as noted in the script, the "rise" cue for actors is
when their names are mentioned.

Lighting can either be up-bright full-stage, or by areas. The
latter is recommended if these technical requirements can be
met, either totally or partially:

Area One:
    Left apron for Bill only, from far Downstage Left to several
    feet toward Center Stage of his lectern
Area Two:
    Upstage Left and Center, lighting Matt's and HST's desks
    and flanking chairs, and several feet Downstage of them
Area Three:
    Center Stage, nearly to Stage Right and Left, and fairly
    far Downstage
Area Four:
    From Upstage to Downstage Right, extending from the sight
    lines to Right Center

Note that HST's affectionate name for his daughter is
"Margie" with a hard "g," not "Marjie."

Bill should speak from all sides of his lectern as his lines
would motivate him to do.

At the discretion of the director, early rehearsals can be
done in Scene—"sketch" fashion, so that the entire company
need not be present at the same time. This will prevent the
hurry-to-wait waste of time, and gain appreciation for the
courtesy of the director.

Chamber/presentational-style theatre allows for improvisation by the director. His inventiveness and the creativity of the cast should be fully utilized. Changes of character through speech, accent, mannerism, and individualities must be accomplished by the actors. Except for Girl, make-up should be from mature to old. Quick lighting cues will aid production pace.

Matt often speaks loudly from his Upstage Left position to actors at Right. While seeming unnatural, this convention works with no loss of credibility.

Playing time is fifty-six minutes for Act One, forty-eight minutes for Act Two, for a total of one hour forty-four minutes—give or take.

Good luck!

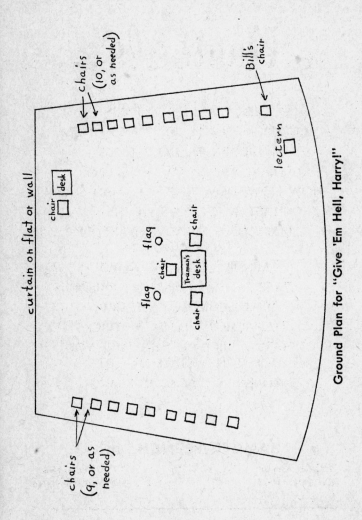

Ground Plan for "Give 'Em Hell, Harry!"

Musicals...

6 RMS RIV VU

BOB RANDALL

(Little Theatre) Comedy

4 Men, 4 Women, Interior

A vacant apartment with a river view is open for inspection by
prospective tenants, and among them are a man and a woman
who have never met before. They are the last to leave and,
when they get ready to depart, they find that the door is locked
and they are shut in. Since they are attractive young people,
they find each other interesting and the fact that both are happily married adds to their delight of mutual, yet obviously sepa-
rate interests.

". . . a Broadway comedy of fun and class, as cheerful as a
rising souffle. A sprightly, happy comedy of charm and humor.
Two people playing out a very vital game of love, an attractive
fantasy with a precious tincture of truth to it."— *N.Y. Times.*
". . . perfectly charming entertainment, sexy, romantic and
funny."—*Women's Wear Daily.*

Royalty, $50–$35

WHO KILLED SANTA CLAUS?

TERENCE FEELY

(All Groups) Thriller

6 Men, 2 Women, Interior

Barbara Love is a popular television 'auntie'. It is Christmas, and
a number of men connected with her are coming to a party.
Her secretary, Connie, is also there. Before they arrive she is
threatened by a disguised voice on her Ansaphone, and is sent
a grotesque 'murdered' doll in a coffin, wearing a dress resem-
bling one of her own. She calls the police, and a handsome
detective arrives. Shortly afterwards her guests follow. It becomes apparent that one of those guests is planning to kill her.
Or is it the strange young man who turns up unexpectedly,
claiming to belong to the publicity department, but unknown to
any of the others?

". . . is a thriller with heaps of suspense, surprises, and nattily
cleaver turns and twists . . . Mr. Feeley is technically highly
skilled in the artificial range of operations, and his dialogue is
brilliantly effective."—The Stage. London.

Royalty, $50–$25

THE SEA HORSE
EDWARD J. MOORE

(Little Theatre) Drama
1 Man, 1 Woman, Interior

It is a play that is, by turns, tender, ribald, funny and suspenseful. Audiences everywhere will take it to their hearts because it is touched with humanity and illuminates with glowing sympathy the complexities of a man-woman relationship. Set in a West Coast waterfront bar, the play is about Harry Bales, a seaman, who, when on shore leave, usually heads for "The Sea Horse," the bar run by Gertrude Blum, the heavy, unsentimental proprietor. Their relationship is purely physical and, as the play begins, they have never confided their private yearnings to each other. But this time Harry has returned with a dream: to buy a charter fishing boat and to have a son by Gertrude. She, in her turn, has made her life one of hard work, by day, and nocturnal love-making; she has encased her heart behind a facade of toughness, utterly devoid of sentimentality, because of a failed marriage. Irwin's play consists in the ritual of "dance" courtship by Harry of Gertrude, as these two outwardly abrasive characters fight, make up, fight again, spin dreams, deflate them, make love and reveal their long locked-up secrets.

"A burst of brilliance!"—*N.Y. Post.* "I was touched close to tears!"—*Village Voice.* "A must! An incredible love story. A beautiful play!"—*Newhouse Newspapers.* "A major new playwright!"—*Variety.*

Copies late fall. ROYALTY, $50–$35

THE AU PAIR MAN
HUGH LEONARD

(Little Theatre) Comedy
1 Man, 1 Woman, Interior

The play concerns a rough Irish bill collector named Hartigan, who becomes a love slave and companion to an English lady named Elizabeth, who lives in a cluttered London town house, which looks more like a museum for a British Empire on which the sun has long set. Even the door bell chimes out the national anthem. Hartigan is immediately conscripted into her service in return for which she agrees to teach him how to be a gentleman rather after the fashion of a reverse Pygmalion. The play is a wild one, and is really the never-ending battle between England and Ireland. Produced to critical acclaim at Lincoln Center's Vivian Beaumont Theatre.

ROYALTY, $50–$35

A Breeze from The Gulf

MART CROWLEY

(Little Theatre) Drama

The author of "The Boys in the Band" takes us on a journey back to a small Mississippi town to watch a 15-year-old boy suffer through adolescence to adulthood and success as a writer. His mother is a frilly southern doll who has nothing to fall back on when her beauty fades. She develops headaches and other physical problems, while the asthmatic son turns to dolls and toys at an age when other boys are turning to sports. The traveling father becomes withdrawn, takes to drink; and mother takes to drugs to kill the pain of the remembrances of things past. She eventually ends in an asylum, and the father in his fumbling way tries to tell the son to live the life he must.

> "The boy is plunged into a world of suffering he didn't create. . . . One of the most electrifying plays I've seen in the past few years . . . Scenes boil and hiss . . . The dialogue goes straight to the heart." Reed, Sunday News.

Royalty, $50–$35

ECHOES

N. RICHARD NASH

(All Groups) Drama
2 Men, 1 Woman, Interior

A young man and woman build a low-keyed paradise of happiness within an asylum, only to have it shattered by the intrusion of the outside world. The two characters search, at times agonizingly to determine the difference between illusion and reality. The effort is lightened at times by moments of shared love and "pretend" games, like decorating Christmas trees that are not really there. The theme of love, vulnerable to the surveillances of the asylum, and the ministrations of the psychiatrist, (a non-speaking part) seems as fragile in the constrained setting as it often is in the outside world.

> ". . . even with the tragic, sombre theme there is a note of hope and possible release and the situations presented specifically also have universal applications to give it strong effect . . . intellectual, but charged with emotion."—Reed.

Royalty, $50–$35

VERONICA'S ROOM
IRA LEVIN
(Little Theatre) Mystery
2 Men, 2 Women, Interior

VERONICA'S ROOM is, in the words of one reviewer, "a chew-up-your-finger-nails thriller-chiller" in which "reality and fantasy are entwined in a totally absorbing spider web of who's-doing-what-to-whom." The heroine of the play is 20-year-old Susan Kerner, a Boston University student who, while dining in a restaurant with Larry Eastwood, a young lawyer, is accosted by a charming elderly Irish couple, Maureen and John Mackey (played on Broadway by Eileen Heckart and Arthur Kennedy). These two are overwhelmed by Susan's almost identical resemblance to Veronica Brabissant, a long-dead daughter of the family for whom they work. Susan and Larry accompany the Mackeys to the Brabissant mansion to see a picture of Veronica, and there, in Veronica's room, which has been preserved as a shrine to her memory, Susan is induced to impersonate Veronica for a few minutes in order to solace the only surviving Brabissant, Veronica's addled sister who lives in the past and believes that Veronica is alive and angry with her. "Just say you're not angry with her," Mrs. Mackey instructs Susan. "It'll be such a blessin' for her!" But once Susan is dressed in Veronica's clothes, and Larry has been escorted downstairs by the Mackeys, Susan finds herself locked in the room and locked in the role of Veronica. Or is she really Veronica, in the year 1935, pretending to be an imaginary Susan?

> The play's twists and turns are, in the words of another critic, "like finding yourself trapped in someone else's nightmare," and "the climax is as jarring as it is surprising." "Neat and elegant thriller."—*Village Voice*.

ROYALTY, $50–$35

MY FAT FRIEND
CHARLES LAURENCE
(Little Theatre) Comedy
3 Men, 1 Woman, Interior

Vicky, who runs a bookshop in Hampstead, is a heavyweight. Inevitably she suffers, good-humouredly enough, the slings and arrows of the two characters who share the flat over the shop; a somewhat glum Scottish youth who works in an au pair capacity, and her lodger, a not-so-young homosexual. When a customer—a handsome bronzed man of thirty—seems attracted to her she resolves she will slim by hook or by crook. Aided by her two friends, hard exercise, diet and a graph, she manages to reduce to a stream-lined version of her former self—only to find that it was her rotundity that attracted the handsome book-buyer in the first place. When, on his return, he finds himself confronted by a sylph his disappointment is only too apparent. The newly slim Vicky is left alone once more, to be consoled (up to a point) by her effeminate lodger.

> "My fat Friend is abundant with laughs."—*Times Newsmagazine*. "If you want to laugh go."—*WCBS-TV*.

ROYALTY, $50–$35

PROMENADE, ALL!

DAVID V. ROBISON

(Little Theatre) Comedy

3 Men, 1 Woman, Interior

Four actors play four successive generations of the same family, as their business grows from manufacturing buttons to a conglomerate of international proportions (in the U.S. their perfume will be called Belle Nuit; but in Paris, Enchanted Evening). The Broadway cast included Richard Backus, Anne Jackson, Eli Wallach and Hume Cronyn. Miss Jackson performed as either mother or grandmother, as called for; and Cronyn and Wallach alternated as fathers and grandfathers; with Backus playing all the roles of youth. There are some excellent cameos to perform, such as the puritanical mother reading the Bible to her son without realizing the sexual innuendoes; or the 90-year-old patriarch who is agreeable to trying an experiment in sexology but is afraid of a heart attack.

"So likeable; jolly and splendidly performed."—*N.Y. Daily News.* "The author has the ability to write amusing lines, and there are many of them."—*N.Y. Post.* "Gives strong, lively actors a chance for some healthy exercise. And what a time they have at it!"—*CBS-TV.*

ROYALTY, $50–$35

ACCOMMODATIONS

NICK HALL

(Little Theatre) Comedy

2 Men, 2 Women, Interior

Lee Schallert, housewife, feeling she may be missing out on something, leaves her husband, Bob, and her suburban home and moves into a two-room Greenwich Village apartment with two roommates. One roommate, Pat, is an aspiring actress, never out of characters or costumes, but, through an agency mix up, the other roommate is a serious, young, graduate student—male. The ensuing complications make a hysterical evening.

"An amusing study of marital and human relations . . . a gem . . . It ranks as one of the funniest ever staged."—*Labor Herald.* "The audience at Limestone Valley Dinner Theater laughed at "Accommodations" until it hurt."—*News American.* "Superior theater, frivolous, perhaps, but nonetheless superior. It is light comedy at its best."—*The Sun, Baltimore.*

ROYALTY, $50–25

THE GOOD DOCTOR
NEIL SIMON

(All Groups) Comedy

2 Men, 3 Women. Various settings.

With Christopher Plummer in the role of the Writer, we are introduced to a composite of Neil Simon and Anton Chekhov, from whose short stories Simon adapted the capital vignettes of this collection. Frances Sternhagen played, among other parts, that of a harridan who storms a bank and upbraids the manager for his gout and lack of money. A father takes his son to a house where he will be initiated into the mysteries of sex, only to relent at the last moment, and leave the boy more perplexed than ever. In another sketch a crafty seducer goes to work on a wedded woman, only to realize that the woman has been in command from the first overture. Let us not forget the classic tale of a man who offers to drown himself for three rubles. The stories are droll, the portraits affectionate, the humor infectious, and the fun unending.

"As smoothly polished a piece of work as we're likely to see all season."—*N.Y. Daily News.* "A great deal of warmth and humor —vaudevillian humor—in his retelling of these Chekhovian tales."—*Newhouse Newspapers.* "There is much fun here . . . Mr. Simon's comic fancy is admirable."—*N.Y. Times.*

$1.75 (Music available. Write for particulars.)
ROYALTY, $50–$35

The Prisoner of Second Avenue
NEIL SIMON

(All Groups) Comedy

2 Men, 4 Women, Interior

Mel is a well-paid executive of a fancy New York company which has suddenly hit the skids and started to pare the payroll. Anxiety doesn't help; Mel, too, gets the ax. His wife takes a job to tide them over, then she too is sacked. As if this weren't enough, Mel is fighting a losing battle with the very environs of life. Polluted air is killing everything that grows on his terrace; the walls of the high-rise apartment are paper-thin, so that the private lives of a pair of German stewardesses next door are open books to him; the apartment is burgled; and his psychiatrist dies with $23,000 of his money. Mel does the only thing left for him to do: he has a nervous breakdown. It is on recovery that we come to esteem him all the more. For Mel and his wife and people like them have the resilience, the grit to survive.

"Now all this, mind you, is presented primarily in humorous terms."—*N.Y. Daily News.* "A gift for taking a grave subject and, without losing sight of its basic seriousness, treating it with hearty but sympathetic humor . . . A talent for writing a wonderfully funny line . . . full of humor and intelligence . . . Fine fun."—*N.Y. Post.* "Creates an atmosphere of casual cataclysm, and everyday urban purgatory of copelessness from which laughter seems to be released like vapor from the city's manholes."—*Time.*

$1.75. ROYALTY, $50–$35